How To Find The Treasures of the Knights of The Golden Circle

By Noted Historian and Treasure Hunter

Dr. Roy William Roush, Ph.D

Published by Front Line Press

Copyright July 2005
ISBN: 0-9723072-7-3

Printed in the United States of America

Copies of this book can be ordered from Front Line Press
Phone (818) 888-5416
or from the Website: KnightsofTheGoldenCircle.net

All rights reserved. No part of this book may be used, reproduced, photocopied, stored in any retrieval system, recorded, or transmitted by any means whatsoever without written permission from the author or publisher, except for brief quotes or excerpts for reviews, provided proper credit is given.

*** NOTICE ***

The publisher cannot verify the authenticity or validity of all information contained herein. All exploration should also be accompanied by individual research. And always respect the property rights of others by gaining permission before going onto private land.

Other Credits of Dr. Roy William Roush

Author of "*Open Fire*", a major 707-page story of personal, front line combat with the Marine Corps during the epic battles of Guadalcanal, Tarawa, Saipan and Tinian in the South Pacific during World War II against the Japanese. The book was awarded the "Best Non-fiction Book of 2004" by the Book Publists of Southern California. Author is also seen describing the combat being shown on the best selling video game "Medal of Honor--The Rising Sun," and "The Assault on Tarawa" by Electronic Arts Entertainments.

Also author of: *The Mysterious and Secret Order of the Knights of the Golden Circle: Lost Treasure Secrets*; and *Fugitives from Freedom*.

Columnist, feature story writer and staff member of: *Treasure; Treasure Search; Treasure Found; Treasure Diver; Treasure Hunter; Treasure News;* and *The CB Guide*.

Co-editor and feature writer: *Treasure Hunter Confidential Newsletter*.
Contributing editor: *Biblical and American Archeologist Newsletter*.
Editor: *Adventures' Club News of Los Angeles*.
Columnist and reporter: The Kansas City Star; *Rocky Mountain Aviation Magazine*; *Fabulous Las Vegas Magazine; Stillwater News Press;* and *the O'Collegian*.

Technical writer for Aerospace Companies for 27 years.
Professor: UCLA and Los Angeles City Colleges.
Featured in: *The Treasure of Elysian Park* on the Television Series "Unsolved Mysteries" --Also on John Burrud's *Treasure Series* --On NBC's Special on *Diving For Spanish Treasure Galleons in Varacruz, Mexico* --On ABC's Series on *How to Find Lost Treasures* and *The Hunt for Amazing Treasures*
--*Treasure Hunters in Search of 17 Tons of Gold*, filmed by the Tokyo Broadcasting System --And the Frank Sayer Show on *The Lost Dutchman Mine* --Plus numerous other radio and television newscasts.

BA, Journalism

Ph.D in Biblical Archaeology.

Dedication

I dedicate this book to all my fellow treasure hunters everywhere--to those of us who will forever be young at heart and in spirit, for we will always follow that big rainbow in the sky for the promise of gold and fortune at its end—and to be sure, my friends, some of it is out there waiting to be found.

Also, to two of my old treasure hunting partners who are no longer with us, Colonel Gordon "Gordo" Cooper, one of the Original Seven "Right Stuff" Mercury Astronauts who set many unbroken world records in space, and was the best fighter pilot I ever flew with--and to Steve Ryland, owner of Cal-Gold and Pro-Mack-South treasure and gold prospecting shops.

Also to my brother, Donald, in Dallas who is also a treasure hunter. And thanks to my wife, Lydia, for her patience while writing another book.

Contents

Other Credits of Dr. Roy William Roush
Dedication

Chapt 1. BACKGROUND ON THE TREASURE HUNTER CONFIDENTIAL NEWSLETTER.....1

Chapt 2. INTRODUCTION TO THE KNIGHTS OF THE GOLDEN CIRCLE 3

Chapt 3. TREASURE HUNTER CONFIDENTIAL NEWSLETTERS FROM APRIL, 1990 TO DECEMBER, 1993 7
Knights of the Golden Circle..7
The Circle Map Overlay   9
The Circle Map Usage..10
Knights of the Golden Circle Treasure Locations..12
More on the knights of the Golden Circle..15
An Interview With James Woodson...16
Knights of the Golden Circle Update...19
Knights of the Golden Circle Treasure Sites Revealed..20
Was the Golden Circle a Circle of Bologna...23
Knights of the Golden Circle Treasure Trove Uncovered..24
Follow Up On Knights of the Golden Circle Recovery 27

Chapt 4. TREASURE HUNTER CONFIDENTIAL NEWSLETTERS FROM JULY, 1995 TO NOVEMBER, 1997 29
Was Jesse James One Of His Names 29
More Background On Jesse James..29
Jesse James Was His Only Name..30
O.J. Was Innocent - Jessie James Third –Guilty?...32
Tom Markwell Shares a Treasure Lead...34
Knights Of The Golden Circle Signs..36
FMDAC Meeting in Tulsa and a Trip To Knights Of The Golden Circle Treasure Sites 36
Drawing of a Double Bent Tree and a Hand Made Diamond-Shaped Marker Stone.......................40
KGC Symbols, Or What?..43

Chapt 5. TREASURE HUNTER CONFIDENTIAL NEWSLETTERS FROM MAY, 1998 TO OCTOBER, 2001 45
To THC, or Not To THC?...45
Jesse James Remains Mysterious 48
Found! Jesse James's Two Million Dollars Keechi Hills Gold Hoard..50
Reader's Roundtable..54
KGC Treasure Cavern Found..55
Discussion With Mike Walsh On The KGC...55
The Truth About the KGC...56
Origins Of The KGC...56

KGC Bibliography 59
Editorial – What Happened To THC??? (Steve's Three Mysterious Visitors) 61
The Real KGC – Conclusion 63

Chapt 6. IS THE FAMOUS LUE TREASURE MAP PART OF THE KGC TREASURE? 65
Karl von Mueller 65
The Incredible LUE Treasure Map 67
The Symbols On The Map—Are They Masonic? 68
A LUE Map Overlay 69
Sketch Of Black Lake Wash 71
Death Traps 72
The Mysterious Death Of Noted Treasure Hunter, Frank Fish 72
Is The LUE Map Associated With The Constellations? 74

Chapt 7. UPDATE ON RECENT SEARCHES FOR THE KGC TREASURES 75
A Letter To The Q&A Department 76
KGC Treasure Believed At Wapanuca, Oklahoma 77
Conclusion 79

Chapter One

Background On The *"Treasure Hunter Confidential Newsletter"*

Without a doubt, the "Treasure Hunter Confidential Newsletter" for the 17 years that it was published, was the finest publication on the subject of treasure hunting and associated information. That's why many people paid $100 a year for it. It was meant for the professional and serious treasure hunters, but was also good reading for the armchair readers.

The publication was by subscription only and was mailed out each month to the subscribers. It never appeared on any of the newsstands. In that way, the subscribers would to be the first and the only ones to know about this valuable firsthand and confidential information. Also, in order not to be influenced by manufacturers or others promoting a product, the publication never accepted any advertising; therefore the writer could give unbiased information and reports as he saw them.

The newsletter carried proprietary stories and information (most printed for the very first time, and normally not found elsewhere) on many known and unknown lost, buried and sunken treasures, including: The Lost Dutchman; Doc Noss and the Victorio Peak Treasure; the Mexican Nationals 17 Tons of Gold in New Mexico; Kokoweef; Beal Code; Caballo Mountains; Oak Island; Cocos Island; Yamashitas Gold in the Philippines; and especially about the treasures of the Nights of The Golden Circle (KGC). Also, there was much general information ranging from archaeology and metal detectors to dowsing, and other useful information.

Its articles about the KGC preceded, by far, any mention in any other treasure publication. In fact, some subscribers (names withheld) wrote in to say that they had used some of this information to successfully find some of their treasure.

It was originated in December 1989 by Larry Williams from Rancho Santa Fe, California. With the instincts of a detective, he had a great talent for accumulating his information. While he wasn't on his job of working with the stock market, he was very active out in the field-- including trips to Mexico, Egypt, Israel, and Saudi Arabia.

Then in 1992, Steve Ryland and myself took over the publication until February 2002, when the publication ceased. However, back issues are still available for $8.00 each, or bound copies of each year for $85. The latest index was in August 1998, Volume 14, Number 8. Any issue can be ordered by contacting Cal-Gold, at 2569 E. Colorado Blvd, Pasadena, CA 91107. Phone (626) 792-6161.

Chapter Two

Introduction to The Knights of The Golden Circle

The history of this secret and little known order of The Knights of the Golden Circle (KGC) is one of the most incredible untold stories in American history today. It's hard to explain why so little is known about it now since it was a very large, important and active organization for many years before and after the Civil War. Their membership was in the thousands and many were also important leaders in social, civic, church and educational systems.

But, their story has somehow been overlooked in our modern history books…like old news. However, most history books during the Civil War period and a lot of other publications did refer to them at the time. But perhaps, we don't want to hear today that a large percentage of our population refused to accept the South's surrender to the North--but instead, set about with secret and seditious plans to restart the war later and to overthrow our government. They were very adamant about keeping slavery alive and to re-establish the Confederate Union. Those are not popular subjects today, and we just don't want to hear now (or maybe admit) that there were things like armed rebellion and insurrection within our ranks…That's like being un-American. We prefer to think that when the South surrendered, the war was over, but it really wasn't. Remember the old slogan, "The South Shall Rise Again." Well, they really meant it!

The KGC had started many years before the war began with bold plans of imperialism to gain more territory for our growing nation (which brought Texas into the Union), and also with amazing plans to annex Mexico. Later, they became devout believers in the rights of the southern cause and against the North imposing its will against them.

When the Civil War started, they resorted to drastic measures and went underground to oppose the North and the Union Army with secretive and bold actions, including sabotage, infiltration of the Government, and a very efficient spy network. Many top politicians, officials, and men of importance were members. They were so effective that President Lincoln once referred to them as a "Fifth Column" which might have been the original use of the term. There is also reason to believe that they were also involved in the conspiracy to assassinate President Lincoln.

In my previous book in March 2005, *"THE MYSTERIOUS AND SECRET ORDER OF THE KNIGHTS OF THE GOLDEN CIRCLE."* (ISBN: 0-9723072-6-5), Web site: KnightsOfTheGoldenCircle.net, there are references (and even some copied material) from some of those old 1800's articles that explain much about their origins and history, including some information on their treasures. It is most interesting material.

During the Civil War, the KGC strongly supported the southern cause. But when the South surrendered, this group refused to accept the surrender. They considered it as only a temporary cease-fire until they could restart the war again. In fact, even before the war was over, they could see that the South was losing. This was something unacceptable to them, and they immediately began plans for another war.

Some military historians have said that one reason the South lost the war was because they didn't have enough money. That was one thing the KGC did not intend to let happen again. To start another war, they needed to accumulate equipment and a great amount of money—especially money. Through donations, but largely through other ways, including theft, skimming profits from businesses, armed robbery and other means, they started amassing a huge treasure of money, gold and silver bars, gold nuggets, gold dust, coins, jewelry and other valuables to finance their plans. All this they secretly buried in many states throughout the country, but mostly in the Southeastern states, in old mining tunnels, pits and holes that they dug, then assigned armed sentries to protect them from being found.

Some of their treasure may include a wagon load of gold that was hijacked and mysteriously disappeared as it was being transported at the end of the Civil War. Some treasure hunters think that it became part of the KGC treasures. There were also questions about what happened to the money that was in the Confederate treasury; and there is reason to believe that the famous train and bank robber, Jesse James, was a member of the KGC and buried much of his loot as KGC treasure. There is also some reason to believe that he was not really killed by Bob Ford, but lived on for many years under assumed names.

But by the time they had amassed their fortune and supplies, World War One brought an end to their plans. Also, most of them had died off anyway by then. But the treasures they buried, which some have estimated to be worth billions of dollars, is the stuff that dreams are made of to treasure hunters.

The author, who is well-known in the field of treasure hunting, learned of this immense treasure years ago, and through his research has presented this information here--not only bringing out this little known part of American history, but also has provided much information here on the treasures, including some rare and never-before-published treasure maps of some of the treasure sites.

Chapter Three

"Treasure Hunter Confidential Newsletters" From April 1990 To December 1993

The following articles about the KGC are taken (actually reprints) from the "TREASURE HUNTER CONFIDENTIAL NEWSLETTERS" starting in April 1990 during its first year of publication by Editor, Larry Williams. The next two chapters will also carry additional information up to October, 2001. There were also many stories in each issue on other known and unknown lost, buried and sunken treasures, including: The Lost Dutchman; Doc Noss and the Victorio Peak Treasure; the Mexican Nationals 17 Tons of Gold in New Mexico; Kokoweef; Beal Code; Caballo Mountains; Oak Island; Yamashitas Gold in the Philippines; etc; as well as much general information ranging from metal detectors to dowsing, and other very useful information. Keep in mind that many people paid hundreds of dollars for this information.

(NOTICE: I cannot personally confirm any of the following information, though I have no reason to doubt it otherwise. Remember, this is not information that I wrote… I'm only reprinting it here. Roy W. Roush)

KNIGHTS OF THE GOLDEN CIRCLE

April 1990, Volume 2, Issue 4

"Without a doubt, the Spanish found and buried more Gold in America than anyone else. But perhaps, close behind them, are the Knights of the Golden Circle. This legendary group of men essentially represented the financial interests of the South during Civil War time period. This group of individuals that one encyclopedia of southern history claims numbered over 3,000,000 men were far-reaching in their financial impact on that war as well as the development of the United States during reconstruction.

This past week we had an intensive and exhaustive interview with James J. Woodson* who may be the leading authority on the Knights of the Golden Circle, a group who appears to have been involved in the financial support of the Confederacy during the American Civil War.

(*This name is an alias. However, I think I talked to this person many years ago before the THC began publication. If so, the person, whose real name has been lost in my files, lived in the vicinity of Lake Elsinore, CA. I remember that I was impressed with his knowledge of the KGC....Roy W. Roush.)

Depending on who's story you believe, the Knights of the Golden Circle (KGC) were either a short-lived group started by George Bickley in Cincinnati, Ohio or a very well-heeled, powerful group who saw their destiny as that of saving the South, and perhaps America from European bankers and a host of other influences.

Those who subscribe to the second viewpoint, allege the KGC had several major treasure stashes throughout the South and West. There have been rumors among treasure hunting circles that some of these treasure sites have been cracked and vast amounts of wealth have spilled into people's pockets.

In our interview with Woodson, we were finally able to pry out of him what the Knights of the Golden Circle is all about...we'll be detailing with that in other Treasure Hunter letters. More importantly he was kind enough to give us an explanation of the significance of the Circle itself.

<u>On the following pages, you will see the Circle and I'll teach you how it relates to treasure finding.</u>

Each square denotes a large treasure. Each circle represents small caches of Gold, Silver or money buried. Of course, the large, dark box in the center represents the treasure that in Woodson's words is "So fabulous, it would stagger the imagination. Usually these are in less than 30 feet of soil."

The significant point about the circle is that if one can find one or two of the treasures, all the rest come easy. Everything is done on a north/south, east/west axis so if you stumble across one of the treasures, you should be able to follow in a straight line until you come across the other treasure. Based on that heading, the rest of the treasures should tumble into place.

The original scale on the KGC Circle is one inch to the mile, so you should find a comparable scale if you were to find treasures that fit the general pattern seen in the circle. If you can locate two of them, then you know the approximate distance of the rest of the targets.

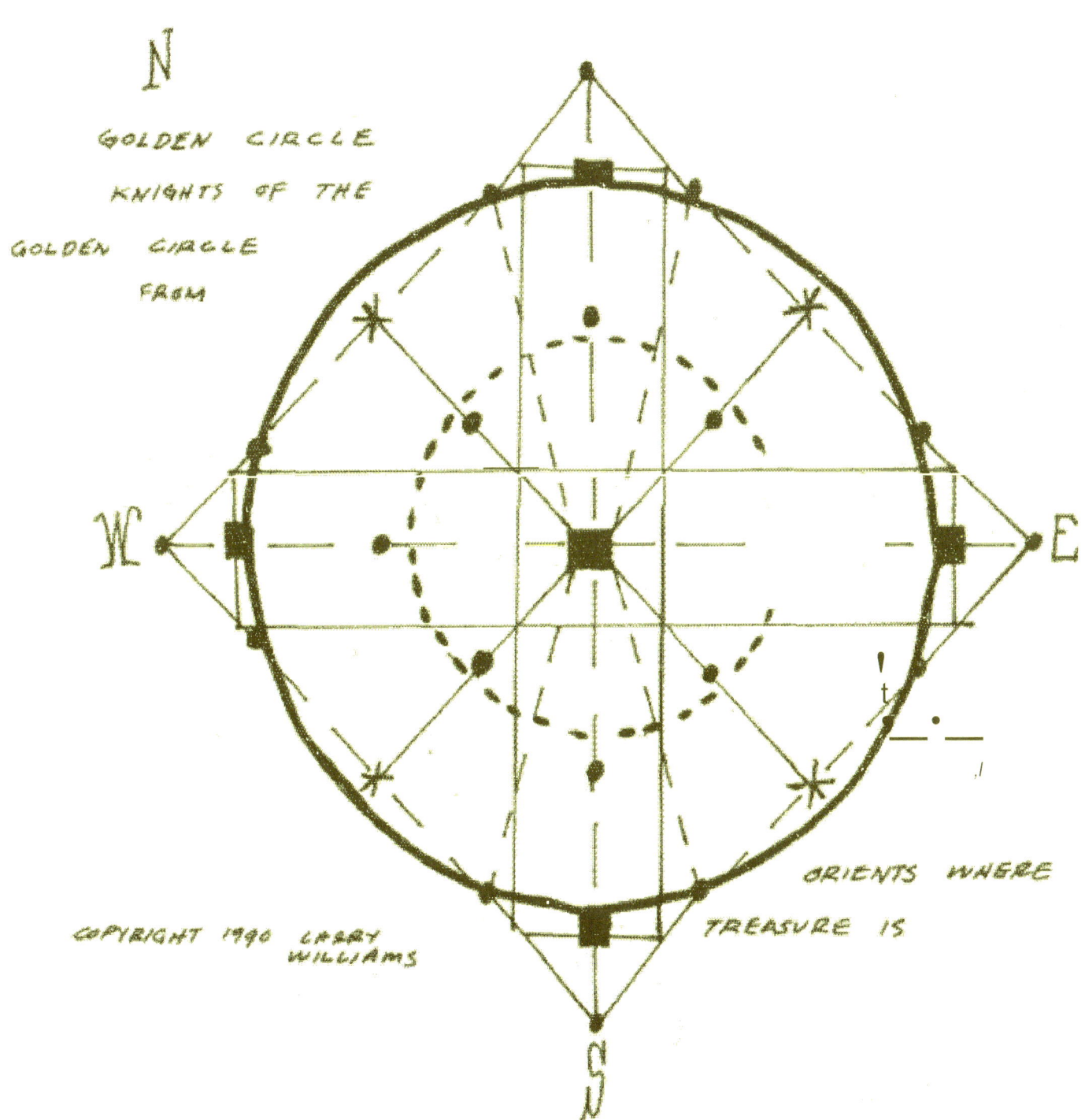

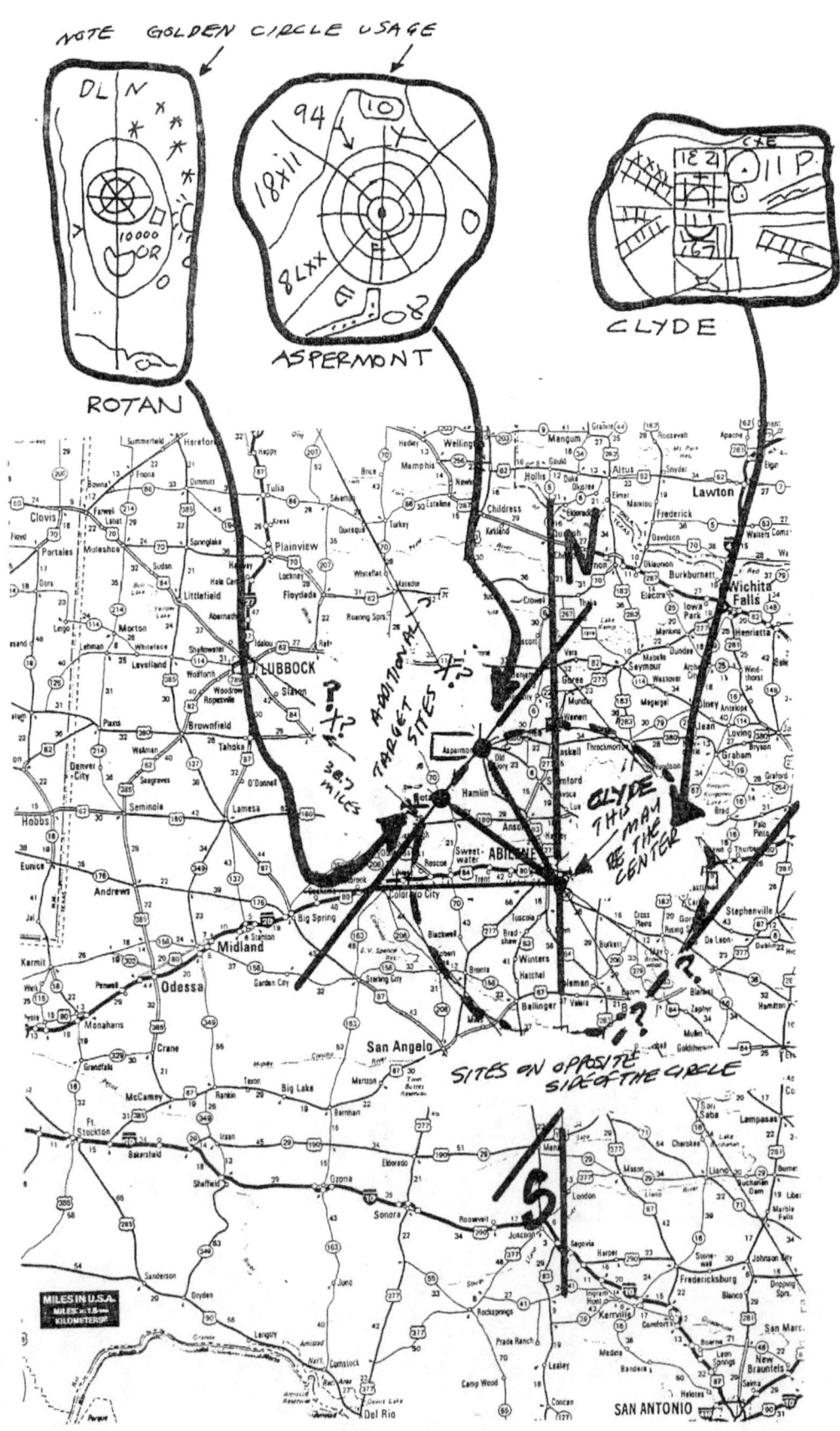

SPINNING A SPIDER WEB

If you look at any of the Spider Rocks, you'll notice a great deal of similarity. You'll see the same north/south orientation, you'll see the same circle with dots. The circles may be squared just as the KGC did.

This may give those of you who want to pursue the Spider Rock treasures a further idea on developing treasure sites.

In fact, when we took the recent "TREASURE MAGAZINE," January 1990 issue, and compared it against the KGC, we saw all sorts of similarities. First of all, it appears that the spider rock stone is turned up-side-down on
the cover of the magazine so we've taken the liberty to redraw it. You can
see some of the things pop into place. Notice the north/south axis of the sun on the east side, which would represent the rising sun. Also, note the location of spider rocks being found in Aspermont, Rotan, and Clyde, Texas by Dave Arnold in the early 1900's. These clearly form one of the vectors of the KGC model!

A point needs to be asked here, are the spider maps KGC, instead of early Spanish? Or did both the Spanish and KGC use a similar code, most likely a Masonic template to hide their treasures? And since the distance from Clyde to Aspermont and Rotan is a ratio of miles, how could this be a Spanish code?

If you think you know where a major treasure site is...such as Victorio Peak...you may want to do some squaring and circling around that area to see what else fits in the map that are in the same north/south, east/west axis or the same vectors coming off the center of the target itself.

I suspect the KGC circle will become an invaluable aid in the South and West as more treasures are uncovered.

We'll be doing an interview with Woodson, as well as reviewing some of the treasures sites that he has run across in his own research of the last many years.

All in all, I probably saw over 250 treasure sites that had been given to Woodson that should make excellent potential trips for subscribers. If we, or our subscribers, could crack just one of these, it would open many, many doors to a substantial amount of treasures right here in America.

Hopefully, we will be able to get more of these target sites from our informant, but for now, we were content with the few he was kind enough to give us. These are primarily in the Oklahoma area, but we did see others in New York, Ohio, as just an example of other states. Hopefully, we will have more of these and they'll be in upcoming issues. I'll have to fill these in for you.

I'll never forget our conversation over an early dinner. (He was more interested in the food.) I was more interested in the reams of paper he had with maps, pictures of how Gold and Silver had been buried showing interlocking tunnels, staircases down, you name it. I felt like a treasure hunter who'd died and gone to heaven.

The gray in his hair and the warble in his voice added additional luster to the stories. At first he was extremely reluctant to make these revelations, but I told him it would be important to him for subscribers of THC to be aware of these treasures.

THE REASON

The reason I told him it is important for our subscribers to know is: If one of our subscribers can find one of these treasures, I feel, and he agrees, there will be more than treasure there. There will be notes and diagrams...most likely in code form...that will link up to additional treasures.

If you're fortunate enough to hit pay dirt with the treasure sites listed below, be very careful with your diggings and don't disrupt anything. Take careful notes of the way things look. If things are in buckets or pails, what direction are they facing - up-down, north/south, east/west? You may even want to take photographs prior to any actual recovery. Of course, if there are any papers, writings, drawings on rocks, etc. please...please...let me know.. Woodson and I will go over them and come back to you and share with you what these additional markings and indications mean. Knocking off just one of these treasure sites should result in several others falling close behind.

Here they go, directly as Woodson told them to me:

KNIGHTS OF THE GOLDEN CIRCLE TREASURE LOCATIONS

<u>Anadarko, OK</u>
Five miles west of Anadarko, Delaware Indians.

Columbus, OH
There are several million dollars worth of gold coins buried on the southeast corner of the State Capital grounds.

Cleveland, OH
Woodson stated emphatically his belief that treasure is buried on the old J. D. Rockefeller estate and on or near the State Capital. The property is well marked by hoot-owl trees or stone work with petroglyph carvings or stone formations. Usually these can be found on the southeast or southwest corner. Look for southeast or southwest bearings to orient yourself.

Helper, Utah
Millions are buried between coalmine #1 and #2, near the Green River. Millions of dollars buried here.

Also in Salt Lake City, a large treasure is supposed to be buried close to the White U painted on the side of the mountain well within the view of the city. This should be a very large treasure and probably has coordinates based on the State Capital.

Caldwell, Idaho
$200,000 is buried on the bluff overlooking Caldwell, Idaho. Also in Boise, Idaho, not far from the old capital building and not far from the old Catholic mission church, a large treasure is buried.

Brownsville, NB
At the old original capital building - go south to a spring along the bluff of the Missouri River and find a large cache.

Davis, OK
At or near the old Indian graveyard, south of Davis, where you cross the Washita River, look under the floor of the old railroad depot in Davis.

Two quart jars of $20.00 gold pieces buried in the fork of the Wild Horse Creek where it empties into the Washita west of Davis.

Rush Springs, OK
At or near the old James farm or homestead there is almost half a million dollars in four or five caches buried along the Little Washita River.

Ada, OK
$50,000 buried in town under tree in front of Dr. Callestsan's house. Also, $1,000,000 is buried near Colgate, at a coal mine near Toka. At Davis, one

should look for an old cemetery. Look for two caches - one at the outskirts of the cemetery and another along the east side. Way back in an old dugout, near a spring, west by southwest of the ranch house is a sizable treasure. Look at the east side of the railroad tracks north of Mulhall.

Salt Lake City, Utah
There is a Knights of the Golden Circle treasure buried in Utah - approximately $100,000.00 - near the capital building in Salt Lake City. There's also a large deposit - over $10,000,000.00 - reported to be buried close to the "U" in the hills not far from the big white "U" representing the state of Utah. There should be co-ordinates with the State Rotunda, not Temple of Mormon. If you find the treasure the "U" will represent utopia and you'd better let me know.

Cotopxi, CO
They put a treasure down on the west side of the bridge across the Arkansas River at edge of the town of Cotopxi.

Mobile, OK
Old Grist Mill	$15,500
Cemetery	$1,250.00
Livery stable	$20,000
City park	$10,000

Durwood, OK
$45,000 southwest of the cemetery 100 yards.

Ardmore, OK
Big treasure one mile northeast of downtown in a rocky, wooded area. Spikes and marks on trees.

Oklahoma City, OK
$50,000,000 southeast of the capital. Really a big one. 12 or 14-feet deep near a popular theatre near the main livery stable.

Paris, TX
Large treasure buried close to an old railroad depot, between the depot and Kyle's Place.

Columbus, OH
Old coins buried on the southeast part of the State Capital grounds, 15-feet deep.

Paul's Valley, OK

About 1/2 to one mile south of Paul's Valley, there's a graveyard across from a house. There's a lot of money there put down in the well on the northwest side of the old house. It should be down about 18 feet to the bottom of the well; a tree would have been planted there and by now the tree would be 80 to 100 years old, so it may not be there. The amount of money involved could be $1,000,000 face value at the time.

Orlando, OK

Three treasures, two in town, one in a cave south of town on the east side of the highway along the Santa Fe Railroad. Look under old rock foundation ruins of a big house. Look next door to the bank on the east side of the old bank building.

REVEALING THE WEB

Notice that three spider rocks have been found in Texas. One is at Aspermont, one at Rotan and one at Clyde. These are three known entities. Notice how they vector in, suggesting the possibility of a major site of buried treasure in the area of Clyde. It could be that the Aspermont and Rotan sites are on the inner circle of the model.

If, in fact, there is a major depository in the vicinity of Clyde, which just seems to be suggested, you can overlay the circle and the square yourself... I've done part of it for you, so you can see where else you should find buried treasure. Note your north/south, east/west axis for potential depositories. A good question would be, are Rotan and Aspermont on the inner circle or the outer circle? The answer to that is not too difficult to define.

If you go out on the same vectors as the Aspermont and Rotan stones an additional 38.7 miles, you should also find either treasure or more Spider Rocks. This would be the area where we feel one is most apt to find additional rocks, in the same vectors coming off Clyde going through Rotan. And, if anything is there, you've got to complete a wheel or Golden Circle in place. If any subscribers are particularly interested in this site, let us know and we'll gladly give you more information.

We don't want to bore the rest of the subscribers with the mundane and arcane, but we feel the information here can most likely be applied to all treasure sites especially anything Spanish or anything involved with KGC.

MORE ON THE KNIGHTS OF THE GOLDEN CIRCLE
May 1990, Volume 2, Issue 5

There may be a treasure site or two, but primarily we'll give you more historical and background info that might put treasure stories in your area into perspective.

Sunday night a subscriber called who said he had made two tentative locations, based on the information in last months story about the Knights. He got good - strong readings, based on a long range detector he used right in the areas we had mentioned!

AN INTERVIEW WITH JAMES WOODSON
June 1990, Volume 2, Issue 6

For you history buffs, here's a bit of my interview with James Woodson, probably the greatest living authority on this obscure, but powerful group of men. I'll dole out more of the interview later in the year.

Q. What was the significance of the Circle?

A. What we're talking about is that there is an Outer Circle, an Inner Circle, and a Golden Circle. The Inner Circle was an organization of appointments. In other words, you had to be appointed through election to become a member of the Inner Circle. To my knowledge, the primary purpose of the Inner Circle was:

1. The perpetuation of the Civil War

2. To control all of the monies that the Outer Circle and the Golden Circle contributed to the organization. They controlled the monies and funds. Those funds were depositories sometimes created long in advance of the need for them. The depositories were established not just with Gold and Silver, but with arms and clothing as well - anything that had any military value. Believe it or not, they even had stashes of certain woods or bars of brass and copper at some places.

Q. Any names you recall?

A. Yes, some of the pre-Civil War names: Sam Houston, Colonel Travis - the head of the Alamo, Colonel George James - the leader of the Confederate army of that era (at the first part of the Civil War) at Fort Sumter, the Moffitt brothers of

California, the mining barons.

Q. Why were these people active in the North?

A. I have to believe that pre-Civil War, there were actually some northern people who were involved in the northern conspiracy against the South that were even active in the Knights of the Golden Circle.

In other words, at one time, this wasn't strictly a Confederate organization. The Knights of the Golden Circle was actually an international organization that included a lot the aristocratic brotherhood of this organization structured it so that these teams, or Knights, established castles.

Now, these castles were actually territories that these men were going to rule. It was their original intention to overthrow the Colonial system of the United States, Canada and Central and South America and to establish this system of teams and castles, where every king was designated a certain amount of territory.

Q. That's why you think castles, now, are significant?

A. Yes, because this is one of the ways that I locate these elder Knights. In order for them to establish their kingdom, they had to build a castle. Then they had just so much territory that went along with this castle. They had all the space split up - Cuba, all the islands of the Caribbean, Central America, Canada. All this was split up into specific territories.

Q. Where are actual examples of these castles?

A. Hearst was established in California. Johnson of Death Valley was established south of the Death Valley area. Senator Clark of Montana was established in the Montana area. I find these castles all over the United States where men were establishing their bases.

They didn't necessarily bury treasures under their castles. The purpose of the castles was to establish a headquarters for themselves. They did this through achievement.

In other words, you achieved becoming a king, you reigned over your castle, and you were still part of the overall organization. You participated financially in the organization, you gave profits to the organization and as a result of that, you got to use all the facilities of the organization ~ other companies, other men, other railroads, other businesses that were established by the organization. All these businesses and kingdoms and castles were all participating. They were all paying a return back to the organization, which the Inner Circle controlled.

Q. What other documentation is there on the Knights?

A. The "Confederate Agent" is a good source. That's the story of the Northern conspiracy and is about a spy who overthrew it for the Northern government. He actually infiltrated it to the point where he got to know some of the heads of the castles and discovered their secret handshake, signs and symbols. Through that information, they arrested the leaders. The government actually destroyed the inner part of the organization in the northeast. That was just about the start of the Civil War or just prior to it.

Q. Let me go back to the Circle for just a minute. You say the Outer Circle got there by deed, the Inner Circle by election, and the Golden Circle by some really major achievement?

A. Right. In other words, you could go from the Outer Circle to the Golden Circle, but that wouldn't necessarily qualify you to become an Inner Circle member.

Q. You could go from Outer to Golden?

A. Exactly. In order to become an Inner Circle member after the Civil War, you obviously had to be a Southerner. You had to be within the qualifications, which were many. One is you had to be an ex-confederate fighter.

Q. Did you have to be white?

A. Oh, no. They did have a lot of sympathy and support from the blacks and the Orientals. So they supposedly started the original Ku Klux Klan, which was started as a military arm of the Golden Circle. It was primarily composed of blacks, Orientals and Indians. Then it converted over the years and turned on the blacks.

Q. How many treasures are you aware of that the Knights of the Golden Circle deposited, where you've gotten specific data on yourself? A couple of hundred?

A. Probably. I understand they had them everywhere on the trails. They put them in strategic locations so that at any time, at the start of the second Civil War, they would be available to people within the organization who knew the codes, signs, and symbols.

Q. I've heard they had treasures in every state, or what we now know as every state, and territory. True?

A. That's what I understand, too. In fact, some of the states have a lot more than others. Obviously, Texas was probably the biggest one.

Q. Other particular states? Oklahoma? California?

A. Mostly, I would say, the states that have the most treasures would be Texas, Oklahoma, and the southern states - primarily because these were the areas these men grew up in and knew the best.

Serious students of this group of Civil War activists may want to read Charles Leland's article about them in the 1862 magazine CONTINENTAL MONTHLY (available at most large libraries on microfilm), J. W. Comfrey's "True Disclosure and Exposition of the Knights of the Knights of the Golden Circle, the Copperhead Conspiracy in the Northwest" by the Union Congressional Committee, and "The Knights of the Golden Circle" by Leonard Waitman (a good account of the Knights' activities in California.)

All of these authors establish the organization as real and sizeable. But since it was a very secret society, it is difficult to estimate just how vast the Knights were.

We have been able to gamer bits and pieces about this group from several sources. As an example, we now know their secret handshake, which is similar to many fraternity handshakes. It consisted of spreading the third and little finger of the right hand and upon shaking hands, inserting this gap between a similar gap on a fellow Knights hand, then saying, "Are you on it?" The correct reply was, "I am on it." Next, you would place your right hand over your pistol and ask, "What's your name?" This was to be answered, "R, A, B, E. Use the letters to spell BEAR...bear flag."

KNIGHTS OF THE GOLDEN CIRCLE UPDATE
June 1992, Volume 4, Issue 6

One of this country's great treasure researchers sent to me the following after reading our articles on the Knights. These notes help establish the validity of the Knights and should highlight our research notes to continue working sites mentioned in their literature.

"This information comes form sources high up in official circles and since it is extremely classified I cannot reveal those sources without endangering their lives and positions. Neither can I grant you the permission to use my name in conjunction with the information should you unwisely decide to print it. This is intended for your personal use only.

"Between 1981 and 1983, the Army, using 18 special forces personnel and an experimental laser drill bored an access tunnel into the bullion storage chambers under Victoria Peak. My original source says they removed 68,240, forty and sixty Lb. gold bars. A letter, just received, from a still-living golden circle member says 30,000 bars had been transferred to other caches long before this happened.

"It appears that the base commander and high ranking government officials (including several Senators and Congressmen) had dirty hands on this one. We were able to partially track the gold after the Army removed it. It was divided into three parts; one going to a secret complex on the White Sands Base itself, another buried near Elephant Butte Dam in Arizona and the last going to a bank vault in the Netherlands under supervision of the Chase Manhattan Bank.

"We also discovered, that, within two years of this event, all 18 of the Army personnel involved had been individually transferred to other places around the world and all had lost their lives in "accidents."

"The golden circle is dwindling with only 25 members at the last reunion. But, I suspect a counterfeit (Government sting operation) may be in the wings. A word of caution - the "Big Boys" are playing for keeps on KGC gold. Those who find don't tend to live long enough to enjoy. They don't want this loot in private hands. Anyone publicly pursuing KGC is monitored heavily (phone, car, office, etc.)."My other sources say this "recovery" is the only one of the 8 major treasures the gummint men have located. There's 7 more out there still waiting...but other sources tell us they are closely watched by the few remaining KGC members and——gummint men. Lordy, Lordy, what's a hunter to do?

P.S. Tom Walburn, one of my subscribers, sent me the following note: "The KGC does obviously exist, as evidenced by that fine recovery allegedly accomplished in Utah recently"

KNIGHTS OF THE GOLDEN CIRCLE TREASURE SITES REVEALED
January 1993, Volume 5, Issue 1

All sorts of things cross my desk each day...the following list of treasure sites from the Knights of the Golden Circle, sure got my attention as several of these sites are ones I have seen the original manuscripts on, so I suspect the rest of the sites are equally valid. The list does not have an author or source on it, so here it is for your perusal...enjoy!

In several of the old Spanish Mission cemeteries in and around San Antonio, several KGC treasures caches were hidden.

In the Ghost Town of Calico, which is located several miles east of Barstow, KGC members hid a large amount of stolen gold bars in a grove of cottonwood trees.

Located somewhere along the Salinas River between Chular and Gonzales, is a large steel safe filled with a treasure of gold dust, bars and nuggets. This safe was stolen by a group of KGC members, but it proved too tough to open, so it was buried in place. (I think this was recovered 2 years ago!)

In Los Angeles, near the Hollywood Bowl and along the present Hollywood Freeway, is hidden a rich KGC treasure valued at several million dollars. This cache is hidden in a concealed cave that is located across from the Hollywood Bowl along a frontage road. I went past this place a few months ago and the area where I believe the concealed cave is, is still bare, but the area is filled in with apartments around it.

Here's some more information on the Knights of the Golden Circle as well:

The Knights of the Golden Circle were formed during the Civil War by a group of the Confederate elite. It consisted of an "Outer Circle" which contained the vast majority of its participants and a 12 member ruling council which was called "the Inner Circle."

Some of the men making up the original Inner Circle were such famous historical figures as Jefferson Davis (President of the Confederacy); the famous Rebel cavalry leader Nathan Bedford Forrest; Governor Crittenden of Missouri; the notorious guerilla leader William Clarke Quantrill; General Joe Shelby (who took his troop of the "Iron Brigade" into Mexico at the end of the Civil war rather than surrender); Frank and Jesse James; Nathan White;

and others.

The members of the Golden Circle appear to all have been Scottish Rite Masons and did not subscribe to the popular belief that the Civil War was fought over the issues of slavery or states rights.

The Knights of the Golden Circle, instead saw the Civil War as a "behind-the-scenes struggle" between Northern bankers and the Southern wealthy for the "financial control of the South" for which the South was ill prepared. Thus realizing early in the Civil War that the Confederacy could not win, the Knights of the Golden Circle began laying the "financial foundation for a second Civil War and an ultimate victory."

A vast network of spies was created and began infiltrating into all levels of the Northern business, military, politics and government. Their goal was to obtain and conceal large amounts of gold, silver, platinum and weapons to be used to fight the "second Civil War."

The so-called James gang and others (they saw themselves not as outlaws but as undercover Confederate soldiers still fighting for their country) used the information obtained from the "assorted spy rings" to steal precious metals and other valuables that were either owned or insured by Northern bankers.

The stolen monies were then re-invested into many business ventures, such as mining, railroads, shipping, etc. Thus, huge fortunes were amassed over the years and then was eventually converted back into gold, silver and platinum bullion before being carefully hidden in over 550 locations all over the original 48 states.

There are, or were, many smaller Golden Circle treasure caches, valued from a few hundred thousand dollars to a few million dollars, left behind in every state. It is believed that most of the treasure caches are still intact.

There is a super-depository in Colorado that is covered with several thousand tons of rock due to a prospector tripping a booby-trap while trying to find the right entrance into the underground storage bunker. One super-depository in Montana is covered by a 40-foot deep lake which was deliberately built to keep others out.

However, operations to acquire more precious metal bullion and other treasures officially ceased and all the treasure caches were sealed for good in
1922 as the ageing and rapidly dwindling survivors finally accepted the reality that the "long planned and prepared second Civil War" was not
going to occur in their lifetime. (It is believed that the current

membership of the Knights of the Golden Circle will die in this generation as all are "direct descendants of the original Knights.)

To protect many of the Golden Circle treasure caches from being pilfered by unauthorized persons, the Golden Circle constructed many booby-traps of black powder and water pressure to protect the hidden treasure sites. The treasure site that has "booby-traps" will be marked with a "red hand" warning. Treasure caches that are not booby-trapped will be marked with two "black hands."

Only certain members of the Knights of the Golden Circle ever knew the exact locations of the treasure caches located in the original 48 states and fewer yet knew how to open the booby-trapped treasure caches safely.

WAS THE GOLDEN CIRCLE A CIRCLE OF BOLOGNA?
February 1993, Volume 5, Issue 2

Our stories on the Knights of the Golden Circle have got you guys off your haunches and writing us letters. Good, and thanks! Here are some of the comments:

"If you feel the stories are valid please explore more. The only two sources of KGC info comes from your letters and the book, "Jesse James Was One of His Names." Are there other sources?

Yes there are.

Almost any Civil War history book will refer to the Knights, but seldom to the extent we have reported on, or the family claiming lineage to Jesse James has talked about. There are a few other sources; many of the true believers have died. I have been fortunate enough to know a good hunting buddy who got obsessed with the KGC many years ago and went to as many sources as he could to validate the stories, especially the ones the Jesse James clan had spread around.

I have seen hand drawn maps and written descriptions of these stories. All in all, I guess I've seen 30 to 50 treasure stories and while most are clearly in the same hand, several others are not. On the surface it appears there is some substance to these stories.

But the stories themselves detract from the credence of the major story. The book mentioned above claims so many treasures, one has got to question the validity of the thesis. The book claims such treasures await us as $630,000,000 in New Mexico, $413,000,000 in Georgia, and $330,000,000 in both Arizona and Nevada. Oh...I almost forgot to add the $2.5 billion in Canada

Mmmmmmmm,.....I wonder was there ever this much gold? And, if so, why did not the KGC carry the day, or at least just buy it outright, during their Civil War quest for victory? Come to think of it, who would care about the outcome if you had that kind of money?

My point is that it seems to me that the KGC was for real. But the size of their gang and treasures has been greatly overstated and promoted. I well remember visiting one of the supposedly largest and most secret in Montana. The supposed treasure is now covered by a lake, but KGC notes and talks tell us just about where the treasure was placed, if it was.

My visit to the site was a flop. Not only did we get no indication of the treasure, but there were no visible roads or old paths that were supposed to be there to haul in the gold.

The other side of the coin comes from a letter a subscriber sent. His cogent comments should be read:

"I was born in Austin, Texas, raised in San Antonio and am very familiar with the Missions you mentioned from the KGC, January 1993 letter. According to a treasure hunting friend of mine, the 27 mule loads of Gold was also known as the "Rock Pens" because this was where the treasure was buried in the Carrizo Springs, Texas area. It was found supposedly some 30 years ago on the QT which is a rule we all live by. When something is found only the folks involved know where and when, that way you don't have taken away that which you have found. That does happen to loud mouths."

KNIGHTS OF THE GOLDEN CIRCLE TREASURE TROVE UNCOVERED
November 1995, Volume 8, Issue 11

This should get the historians as well as treasure hunters buzzing:

Two long time subscribers called me over a month ago to tell me they felt they were "about on top" of a Knight of the Golden Circle treasure. They told me they thought it was a huge treasure trove worth millions of dollars based on the maps they had acquired from a now deceased son of a man who claimed to be a KGC'er.

For years, people in Southern Utah had heard the old gents stories, most wrote them off as a retired mans hallucinations. Granted, a local newspaper did an article on his story. But, as the good book says, there were not many believers.

Our subs were prompted by the article and began their search over 6 years ago. They tried everything from witching sticks to MFD machines to locate the trove. Several times, they told me, they knew they were right onto it but their diggings produced nothing, other than the need for some Ben Gay, Advil, or Jack Daniels.

This is the most unusual part of their story...around the spot where they eventually found the treasure they had six empty digs. That means six times their equipment was excited, or attracted, by something. A line connecting the dry holes forms more or less a 6-sided figure, as I've indicated below.

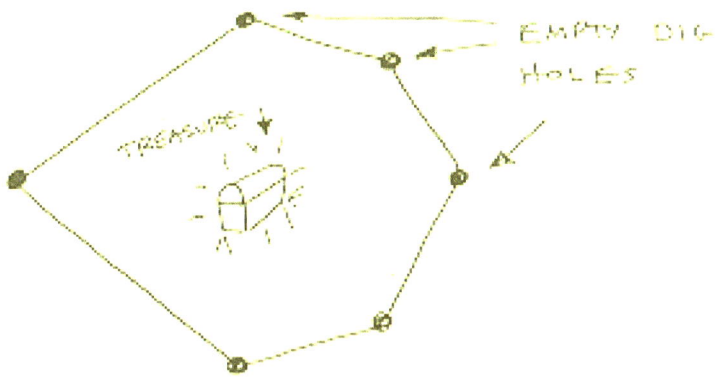

The amazing thing is the eventual treasure was found dead in the middle of this format.

Was something placed out side the treasure...or did something, some energy form...radiate out from the treasure, ala the Walburn Rejection Syndrome we have written about at length in these letters?

The lucky hombres will not tell me how far apart the 6 points are, but I gather they are more than 440 yards. How much more I do not know.

NOW TO THE TREASURE

First, the bad news; the treasure was not worth millions, at least so they say.

The good news is the value is well over $300,000, by today's prices and there have been some snazzy new pick up trucks being driven around the area.

The treasure trove consisted of nuggets, a few small gold bars, some coins (this is where the real value of the treasure was)...and documents. Our intrepid buddies are pleased with their new found wealth, but swear the documents open up other treasure possibilities and shed a very bright light on what the KGC were really all about. So far, they have been very tight lipped. THC is the only publication they have and discuss the project with. I get the impression they will share more as time goes by and they get what they want.

When pressed, they did say the documents do not back up the claims of some that KGC treasures are in every state, and whatever it is they are looking at suggests the treasures are not mega million dollar deals. BUT, treasure is there, that they have proven, and now have reason to believe there's more out there to find.

They kindly said our letters on the KGC diagram is what enabled them to go to the center of the hexagon to find the treasure and to stop looking on the "outside."

I have seen photos of the dig as well as of the objects, and have no reason to think anything has been doctored with.

FOLLOW UP ON KNIGHTS OF THE GOLDEN CIRCLE RECOVERY
December 1993, Volume 5, Issue 12

While other treasure publications write about someone finding an old dime, dollar or class ring, THC, has consistently brought you news of the major real treasure finds of 1993. Last months disclosure of the KGC find in Utah has had many people buzzing. Here's the latest....

Our intrepid treasure finders now tell me they have located the site of another KGC treasure, in the West, based on the papers found along with the coins they uncovered in Utah. The problem they are now having is that while the papers are genuine, in their opinion and all evidence of this newest treasure is there, the location may make it almost impossible to recover.

Strange as it might seem, most of the KGC treasures appear to have been stashed in locations that later became government protected sites, state or fed, thus now making recovery difficult.

Clearly, I am not getting the full story from these lucky (as in hard working) guys...but they are frustrated with the locations of the treasure spots the documents name.

As I read them, and read between the lines, the KGC treasures are not nearly as large as people have thought in the past. In fact they tell me they expect the majority of the treasures will be found to contain around $1,000 in "back then" value. This fits with some of my research, though not all, which suggests the Knights were not as affluent as most authors have made them out to be. It seems each treasure hunting writer has doubled their wealth to the point they had enough money to control the world...so...why didn't they??

Anyway, more data will come foreword from these guys; I hope, as they continue their exploits across the West and back into time. They suspect that KGC booty buried back East is not mentioned in treasures buried in the West, and perhaps vice versa. As 1994 unfolds I hope to get closer to the heart of this matter. "Stay tuned" as they say in Radio Land.

Chapter Four

Newsletters From July 1995 To November 1997

WAS JESSE JAMES ONE OF HIS NAMES??
July 1995, Volume 8, Issue 7

Since publication of the book, "Jesse James Was One of His Names" by Del Schrader, which contends that Jesse James was just a front used by a man who later became a US Senator, there's been a great interest in just who, and or what, Jesse James really was.

We may soon fund out.

Retired Orange County Superior Court Judge, James Ross, and a group of Texans have spearheaded an effort to exhume the body that lies where Jesse James was hurried in 1882. James-names fans say he really died in 1951 at the ripe old age of 107.

A Missouri Judge has granted the request, and exhumation is expected to take place in late July. If the body is the real James, then there's been a whole lot of conning going on for the last two generation of treasure hunters by purported "relatives" of Jesse. We'll stay on top of this one, 'cause if the body is not the real Jesse James, there are far reaching consequences to treasure hunters ... especially concerning the Knights of the Golden Circle. Stay tuned all you happy campers, stay tuned.

MORE BACKGROUND ON JESSE JAMES
August 1995, Volume 8, Issue 8

Thanks to Joyce Dye, we can report the following about the Jesse James exhumation (which has gotten extensive, though not detailed enough, national media coverage.)

Former Texas Attorney General, Wagoner Carr, was at the graveside dig as he believes it's Charlie Bigelow (a member of the James gang) and not the famed outlaw James in the grave.

Carr is saying James resurfaced under the name J. Frank Dalton, turned into a businessman, and eventually acquired part of the Waco-Houston railroad line. Shortly before "Dalton's" death, Carr's theory goes, the then 100-year-old robber revealed his true identity to family members, plus told them his robberies were not for personal gain.

As he explained it, the robberies were meant to bolster the coffers of the Knights of the Golden Circle, a group we have written at length about in the annals of the THC.

This ill-gotten wealth was stashed for financing the war effort the Knights envisioned would some day take place. All but a few of the vaults are hush secrets. One, in the Brazos River, was told to family members, who have tried to recover the treasure. In 1930, an attempt to was made to raise the heavy steel vault. Eyewitnesses claim that the vault was chained and raised partially out of its muddy grave. But, the cables snapped... sending the treasure, or at least a bank safe, back to its murky hiding spot in the river.

I too have heard this same story over the years, so perhaps there is a modicum of truth. Certainly the autopsy will tell us much of what we need to know. Stay tuned. We'll keep you up to date.

JESSE JAMES WAS HIS ONLY NAME
October 1995, Volume 8, Issue 10

For the last 25 years intrepids, historians and treasure hunters have suffered under the delusion that Jesse James was in fact a man of many faces and at least two different death certificates. All this has been perpetrated by two chaps claiming (1) to be the son and grandson of Jesse James (2) to have maps and diagrams leading to great amounts of civil war and Knights of the Golden Circle (KGC) treasure.

Supposedly, Jesse James faked his death, placing the body of Charlie Bigelow in his casket and then skipping off to Texas, taking the name of Henry Ford and acting as a banker. He next moved on to Montana where he assumed the nome-de-plum of William Andrews Clark, becoming one of the legendary Copper Kings. The story continues, as Clark, James amassed a mega-fortune, which he salted away at various sites to be used in the KGC effort.

In the book, "Jesse James Was Just One of His Names," photos of Clark and James are shown, depicting some similarities and an intriguing story is woven across the pages of the dual identity.

It culminates in Clark cashing in his chips and moving to New York City, living in a clandestine Howard Hughes fashion, never to be seen by the pubic again.

All this good information has been provided by Jesse James the third and of more recent, Jesse James the fourth. It seems Jesse James the Second, was a bit of a waste of time, even Jesse kind of blew off his son, preferring the grandson.

Jesse 3 and Jesse 4 have just about milked more money out of treasure hunters and speculators, than slick Willie has extracted from taxpayers. They developed a wonderful scam, "Here's the book that proves Jesse James was dark, proves there was treasure and we are the direct descendants".

The final squeeze, of course, is. "And we have the maps...which we will provide to you, just cross our palm with some shiny stuff or greenbacks...we'll divulge all and split the proceeds with you."

What a story. What a pitch! What a bunch of money they raised from common, decent folks all over this land. I know. Several of my buddies anted up and were given copies or claimed original documents of treasure.

In one instance the purported James clan claimed to have a map showing where Jesse 1 had stashed away the gold taken from Butte, America, the richest hill on earth. Conveniently, of course, a dammed up lake now covers the site. But being no city slicker, I checked all this out for Red Rock Russ and one thing became quite obvious; even if water now covered the treasure (supposedly inside a cave) there could have been only one way to get to this location.

So, instead of diving in the lake or looking for a turtle carved in the rock (that was the key symbol to all the wealth) I looked for a trail to see how and if anyone could have ever gotten into this remote area. What I found was a big bunch of nothing. No trail, and no way to have done what was claimed, which was bringing in hundreds of loads of gold and silver, and only 60-80 years ago. That much tramping around would have left clues, campsites, trails, something. But there was nothing, nothing where there should have been something. Lot's of something!

Funny thing though...none of the James followers ever found any treasure! It's sure as heck not because they failed to try. In one case close to $100,000 was spent funding the supposed James relatives, traveling across hundreds of God's green acres, eating at cheap restaurants and renting broken down old backhoes. Dreams were dreamt and dreamt hard. Holes were dug, and dug deep. All to no avail.

After several years of all this even the truest believer of the James Gang began having their doubts.

Former Texas Attorney General, Waggoner Carr, who represents Jesse Franklin James (the fourth), set the legal wheels in motion to put all this to the acid test. In September, he had the supposed body of Jesse James exhumed from its Missouri burial for the express purpose of doing DNA tests to determine, once and for all, the truth of this issue.

O.J. WAS INNOCENT-- JESSE JAMES THIRD - GUILTY?

While the O.J. jury obviously could not figure out DNA evidence (One juror was quoted out here on morning television as saying, "Ah, all that DNA stuff doesn't mean anything, anyway"), but Waggoner Carr can.

Mark my words on what you are about to read. The treasure "rag mags" will be writing that exhumation took place saying two things were discovered;

First, The body in the grave that's supposed to be Jesse James was placed in the casket face down. Hmmm....The plot starts to thicken.

Next, you'll be told that James Starrs, a forensic expert from George Washington University, stated that "Just about everything historians had believed about James was confirmed by DNA testing. This includes genetic proof that the James family line extended from the outlaw's mother, Zerelda James, right down to living descendants who gave blood samples."

Let me re-state my point...the treasure mags and community will play up this story as gospel, claiming the mystery has been put to rest, that the body in the casket is in fact the one and only Jesse James, face down at that! Hmmm...face down, isn't that supposed to mean something??

But...you pay us 100 clams a year for accuracy as well as advice...and the accuracy of the statement alluded to professor Starrs is not correct. I have personally talked with Waggoner Carr, and was told, "The recent

press release reported from Starrs is in error. Professor Starrs will make no more comments about the facts of this matter until February 23, 1996 at the National Conference on Forensics to be held in Nashville.

"The professor says no information has been released at this time about the DNA, any comments anyone has made or attributed to Starrs is speculative at best."

Attorney Carr did add some cogent points to the discussion. He claims to have read hundreds of documents which we feel establishes some credibility to the James claim. I was told there are three great grandchildren, all in the Waco area, who are pursuing this matter. Carr says he's read over 60 sworn affidavits of people who testified under oath that J. Frank Dalton was in fact another alias of Jesse.

Standard thinking is that Jesse died in 1892, while Carr's clients say he really died at the ripe old age of 107 in 1951, and is buried in the grave of J. Frank Dalton, in Granby, Texas.

In fact, the "family" is so hopped up on this idea that Carr told me, "It doesn't matter what Starrs' work shows, the family will not believe anything until we exhume Daltons grave. That should prove, finally, who is really who in this game of musical caskets."

Carr was originally contacted by the James guys when they felt they were about to recover a treasure. Fearful of having it taken from them by gummint men or landowners they went seeking legal muscle.

This treasure hot spot has now been flooded by the Brazos River, near Waco. Carr has been told it contains close to $4,000,000 of gold and records of where other treasure are to be found. One of my contacts says the records to more treasure make them worth far more than the measly $4 million.

Carr told me, "There was an attempt by Jesse 1 to recover the loot in
1930. Supposedly the vault was broken into and chains were placed around a safe. As it was being raised up the chains broke cutting off a workers foot at the same time.

"In 1965 another attempt was made to lift the treasure up. Again cables snapped, thus the vault sank, probably deeper this time -- into the murky depths. The current attempt to regain what's been lost is now out of money, so...the ultimate resolution remains unknown. I asked Carr, point blank, if any treasury recovery was made and was told, "No."

I pushed it a bit further with the following. "As near as I can tell, there has never been a treasure recovery based on any of the James "family" information. Is that a correct statement?"

He replied, "That's correct. So far, there have been no recoveries anyplace."

Finally, let me say that I too have seen the sworn statements, hundred of pages of treasure maps, diagrams, stories, and the like. At one time, there were several small U-Haul trailers full of such documents and memorabilia. Lots of smoke...but is there any fire?

We'll just have to wait until February 23rd, next year. Even then the debate will go on, until the Frank Dalton grave is exhumed, and we get-- once and for all, a face-up view of the body behind door number two.

TOM MARKWELL SHARES A TREASURE LEAD
August 1996, Volume 12, Issue 8

Hard working Tom Markwell has contributed the following treasure lead for those of you in the Mid-West.

"There is a Jesse James cache in Arkansas that I have known about for over thirty years. I obtained a CD-ROM disk by Stan Grist, titled "LOST TREASURES OF THE WORLD." It told about the James cache, and helped narrow down the area of where the cache is buried. If I wasn't familiar with the area in Arkansas, the information on the CD- ROM wouldn't have meant anything to me, as the spelling of the town, close to the cache, is incorrect.

In 1973, Thomas Penfield published a guide to Arkansas treasures, and mentioned the James cache as being in the Southwestern part of Yell County, Arkansas. Yell is one of the largest counties in Arkansas, with two county seats. Between, the CD-ROM and Penfield's book, I have been able to, more-or-less, pinpoint the general area. Although, I was born in Oklahoma, I lived many years, on and off, in Arkansas. Four, of the caches are associated with the old

Indian trail, and I'm sure there are many more caches along the old trail. Other than knowing where the trail was located, there is no longer any signs of the trail left. The trail has been obliterated by timber logging and farming.

A couple of miles north of the area where the James cache is located, there is an island with a forty-foot-high mound where Hernando DeSoto camped for some period of time. In 1931, around ten thousand dollars worth of artifacts were found. By today's prices, this would amount to around a hundred thousand dollars.

I am sure there are more artifacts since metal detectors weren't available in 1931.

Within, a three-mile radius of the island, there are six caches, including one cache of six jack-loads of gold. Other than the James cache, and the DeSoto camp grounds, none of the other caches have been recorded. They have been passes down by word of mouth from one generation to the next.

As far as I know, I'm the only living person that knows of the caches, since all of the old timers that told me are now gone. This area was near a major Indian trail that led from Mulberry, Arkansas, a junction point, east of Ft. Smith to Hot Springs, and then east to the Mississippi river, and down to New Orleans."

THEN HE ADDS TWO OTHER TID BITS:

"One thing that you might mention in the news letter is the price of Topographical maps have doubled in price during 1996. The DeLORME Mapping Co. has a Street Atlas USA, that not only covers streets, but includes all roads and trails in the U.S. on CD-ROM.

The DeLORME Mapping has other CD-ROMS with professional mapping and contour lines. The maps can be printed out with a multi- media computer, in living color, and they are just as good as the military quadrangle-topographical maps. The address; DELORME MAPPING, P.O. Box 298, Freeport, MA 04032.

The Street Atlas USA can be purchased at SAMS discount warehouse stores, a division of Wal-Mart stores, for around $45.00 dollars.

PS - You might mention in the newsletter that there is a possibility of using multi-frequencies (MF) for creating a tone, for resonating a cache. MF tones are generated by a touch telephone when dialing. It takes two audio generators to generate a MF tone. MF tones are the sound heard when dialing a telephone. Audio Generator is synonymous with function generators, except the function generators have a higher frequency range."

KNIGHTS OF THE GOLDEN CIRCLE SIGNS
September 1997, Volume 13, Number 9

This picture above shows a KGC signpost that was actually used to locate a treasure in the south-central U.S. It is said to have been a big one. I hope it means something to some of you. Can it be very old on a tree that size? We hope to have more of these kinds of things after the Tulsa meeting.

A SPECIAL REPORT ON THE ANNUAL MEETING OF THE FEDERATION OF METAL DETECTOR AND ARCHEOLOGICAL CLUBS IN TULSA AND A TRIP TO KNIGHTS OF THE GOLDEN CIRCLE TREASURE SITES.
(By Roy W. Roush)
October 1997, Volume 13, Number 10

Boy! What a bull session that turned out to be at our special all-day seminar that was held in a penthouse meeting room especially for THC subscribers, Knights of the Golden Circle researchers, and our special guests. This was held immediately after my regularly scheduled 11:00 a.m. address to the FMDAC on the incredible treasures of the Knights of the Golden Circle. It was a bull session to end all bull sessions.

The penthouse meeting room had 30 chairs and they were all full when we started--and it didn't end until after 1:30 a.m. I had already given my information at the 11:00 a.m. address, so I just sat down and shut up (well, mostly) because I wanted to hear what others had to say about the many treasures of the Knights of the Golden Circle, and I learned much more than ever before from these guys.

One of the main contributors was a gentleman who came all the way from southwestern Arkansas. He was a third generation researcher on the KGC and had an enormous scrapbook of photos and stories on the subject and about some of the treasures that have actually been found.

This treasure is perhaps the largest ever hidden in the United States. In fact, there are many, many sites throughout the entire United States where the stuff is hidden. It consists of gold, silver, jewelry and other valuables, plus guns, ammunition, uniforms, and other military equipment. It was buried for many years following the Civil War by southern patriots and soldiers who refused to accept the defeat of the South and consequently planned to restart the war after they were satisfied they had enough financing and equipment to insure victory this time.

It was a secret society with death to anyone who revealed its secrets or where their treasures were hidden. However, their existence was well known and there are countless documents, stories, and articles that still exist which were written about them at the time, mostly from 1864 through 1900. But as large and as important as they were at the time, they were somehow sanitized from our history books today.

So, what happened to them after they had secreted this huge treasure away? Well, their ambitions were ended by the First World War. It united the country, and the group saw that their opportunity had passed, and that very few were in favor of another Civil War by then and they officially disbanded in 1916 without any decision about what to do with the treasure.

But what about all these treasure sites scattered around the country? Most are still there. Some have been found. Some are booby trapped, which makes them dangerous to hunt for.

The treasures of the KGC were mostly discussed, but other treasures were also mentioned, such as: the 17 tons of the Mexican Nationals' gold bars buried in the northwestern part of New Mexico (where I had just returned from last month to do a 1 hour TV special on it); Doc Noss's Victoria Peak treasure (also in New Mexico); loot that Jesse James had buried; as well as other bandit loot;

Spanish treasures and their signs as well as miscellaneous others.

Names of some treasure hunters went as far back as Abe Lincoln, Bill Mahan, Karl von Mueller, Rocky LeGaye, plus a lot of others; both past and present were mentioned. Also the merits of some equipment were discussed.

In the meantime, Steve was trying to hold down our two THC tables in the main convention room. It was full. All of the metal detector manufacturers were there as well as all treasure publications, and other miscellaneous dealers and displayers.

This event was hosted by three of the treasure hunting clubs in the area and with my old friend Bill Huntly (ably assisted by his wife Della Ruth) as coordinators. It was a great success, except for the hard and cold rain on Sunday during the hunts. But it didn't deter any of the contestants and apparently no one dropped out and all tokens and most coins were recovered.

It was nice to see Tulsa again and to hear that soft mixture of both southern and western accents. Also, it's near where I was born (at Alva, Oklahoma) and where I went to school at Oklahoma City and Enid. But I left there in 1942 to join the Marines and didn't spend much time around there until I went back to Stillwater (Oklahoma State University) in 1946 to 1950 for my BA Degree in Journalism. Then it was off to the Air Force where I flew jet fighters during the Korean War.

But I still have some relatives and friends in Tulsa, including one of my favorite cousins, a fraternity brother and a couple of friends--all of whom came to hear my presentation on the treasures of the KGC, so I was among old friends, relatives, and familiar surroundings.

Then Sunday afternoon, I and my friend John Melancon (who owns the treasure shop at Aztec, New Mexico and who figured so prominently in the filming of my one-hour TV special on searching for the 17 tons of gold in New Mexico last month) and my new friend, Bryan Hines, were privileged to be invited by the gentleman from Arkansas to visit numerous locations in southwestern Arkansas and southeastern Oklahoma. Here, we were shown a number of sites where the KGC treasure signs and symbols (called pointers) were located.

These were in the order of purposely-bent trees, when they were much smaller, or sometimes where one tree had been grafted onto another. Also, there were certain types of cryptic letters, numbers, and other figures carved into trunks of some very old trees. These were all done in an especially individualist and artistic manor--unlike anything I had ever personally seen before, except for one time in about 1973 at Glorieta Pass, New Mexico, as I will mention later on. I learned that these pointer locations were in sets of three or four, or more, for each treasure depository--which could be miles away, or very close.

There was a particular pattern that I noticed for all of the sites that I saw. First, there was a double bent tree that could attract your attention from some distance away. And I should point out here that all of these pointer sites were in heavily wooded and hilly areas. The ones we saw were near an old wagon trail or road. In this manner, they could be periodically inspected by the designated sentry for that area. And if he noticed any fresh signs of disturbance or digging, he would wait around for a few days to set up an ambush for whoever might be searching in the area for the treasure, and usually the intruder would be killed if he didn't have an otherwise good excuse for being there.

Then in addition to the bent trees and their markings, there were always some peculiar diamond-shaped rocks--somewhat like the Masonic Emblem (which was not a coincidence). And they were also thick, like a big slice of cake. Then, they would have "witness marks," which were certain notches and niches or signs, like a horse shoe. Usually there were 2 or 3, or more, of these diamond-shaped stones in sizes from 4 or 5 inches long up to maybe 15 or 16 inches long-but always in the same proportions of thickness.

Also there were usually 1 or 2 boot-shaped stones, and all the stones were placed in a certain pattern, like maybe a cross or an X with the tree in the center. All stones were placed an equal distance apart and when you saw 2 or 3 of them you could guess where the others were, and sure enough, there they would be!

Now comes a sinister part. Close to some of the sites was a mound of dirt looking exactly like the fill over a hole where a big treasure had been buried. These were always a fake--to lure an unsuspecting treasure hunter into digging into the site to find treasure--and which consequently would show signs of digging when the KGC sentry made his next inspection, and thereby set the trap for the treasure hunter. Treasure was rarely, if ever, buried close to the marker sites.

Since I had grown up on farms and ranches in this part of the country and did a lot of hunting and fishing; and I consider myself a pretty good woodsman--but I had never seen anything like these sites. They were very, very

easily noticed if you knew what to look for, but otherwise, they blended in with their surroundings so well that they were
almost impossible to notice.

After seeing the first one or two sites, I especially watched for any other bent trees, and only where I saw one of these trees is where we stopped and where the other signs appeared around it. Also, the diamond-shaped stones were seen nowhere else.

Virtually all of the sites we saw were located in the National Forest, which takes up a very large part of that area. This means no metal detecting or digging is allowed so we didn't even have metal detectors along. But I did get a lot of good photos and videos as proof of what I saw.

Now, I have believed in the fabulous treasures of the KGC for many years and in about 1975, I went to a site at Glorietta Pass, New Mexico, to look for one of these treasures. I was only informed to look for signs, which could lead me to the treasure. But I didn't know what sort of signs to look for, so I just kept my eyes open. Eventually, I noticed a bent tree with two 90-degree bends (see drawing). This I knew wasn't natural and could be a sign. Next I discovered a very distinct face carved into the side of a big rock nearby. Then more signs, which I followed, which led me to dig at a certain site on the edge of a large dry wash. Here, I found an old metal black powder can and under it were the remains of an old wooden pay chest--EMPTY! Someone (and I found out later who it was) had beaten me to it by only about 4 months.

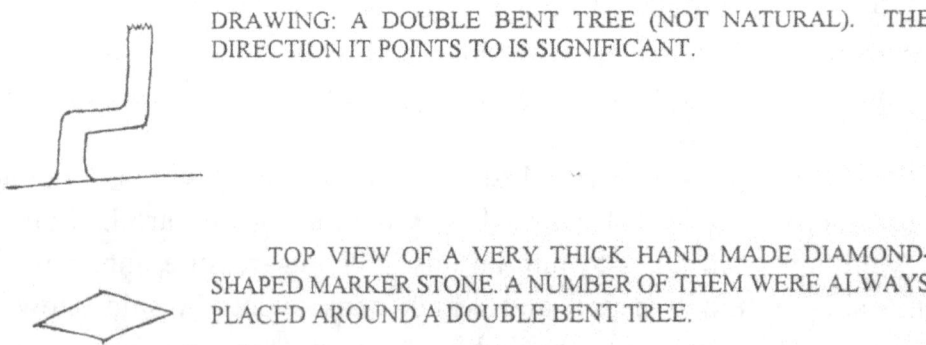

DRAWING: A DOUBLE BENT TREE (NOT NATURAL). THE DIRECTION IT POINTS TO IS SIGNIFICANT.

TOP VIEW OF A VERY THICK HAND MADE DIAMOND-SHAPED MARKER STONE. A NUMBER OF THEM WERE ALWAYS PLACED AROUND A DOUBLE BENT TREE.

That was the only double bent tree that I ever saw until last month in Arkansas and Oklahoma where I saw more of them. I saw and heard of much more evidence of the Knights of the Golden Circle and their treasures, which are too numerous to mention here.

However, the next day, John Melancon and I journeyed up to the flint hills area of southeastern Kansas where I spent most of my summers while I was in grade school. Here, on the edge of the timber, is where my grandparents lived on an old fashioned farm, and the time I spent there was some of the happiest in my life. I had been wanting to go back for years, and also to do some detecting there, which we did, and found only a few old pennies. But the surprise was that on the old farm my grandparents owned, where there was an old creek crossing used by wagons before the bridge was finally put in, I found a bent tree with 4 or 5 of the same type of diamond-shaped rocks around it like we had just seen in Arkansas. It was definitely a pointer site. But we were walking out of the area for the car and I had to catch an airplane in Wichita for home in a few hours so we didn't have any more time to spend there— BUT, I'LL BE BACK!

As I said before, I have believed in the treasures of the KGC for years, but what blows my mind now is the enormity of it.

So, if all of these carefully fashioned double-bent tress and very time consuming diamond-shaped rocks, the elaborate and fancy carvings on trees, and other signs and pointers (which were left virtually throughout the entire United States) are not related to treasure, then you have to believe that there was a horrific amount of time and energy spent by many hundreds of people over a long period of time around the country just to perpetuate a gigantic hoax--which is something I definitely cannot accept. Times were not easy after the Civil War. Making a living was hard and very few people had time to spend on just a hoax of this proportion.

Let me conclude by mentioning that this gentleman expert from Arkansas, whom I have talked to over the phone a few times and also have his booklet and a video tape on this subject, occasionally gives special classes to small selected groups on this treasure and its signs and symbols and what they mean. But he doesn't want to be harassed by the curious or debated by those who doubt the existence of such a treasure.

And you might reasonably wonder then why he would give information and instructions to anyone else, if he truly knew how to understand these signs and symbols that could lead to these treasures. Well, to borrow a phrase, "There are so many treasures, and so little time." He knows of perhaps a hundred or more sites, and he can't possibly follow them all.

KGC SYMBOLS, OR WHAT?
November 1997, Volume 13, Number 11 (By Steve Ryland)

After the FMDAC Convention in Tulsa and the KGC Seminar, the thing that surprised me the most was the extent of KGC symbols and their complexity. One researcher estimated that it might have taken around 15 men several months to maybe a year to complete the symbols for a single depository. That seems like a lot. Although there may be hundreds of signs for each depository or sub-depository, all coherent and surveyed in, it does seem like a long time considering that those in the know ought to be able to figure it out from relatively few signs. I generally have a minimalist attitude on these sorts of things and also have the same sorts of questions regarding some Spanish treasure signs where whole mountains are carved, when time could be better spent mining.

Now, don't get me wrong. I know there are KGC signs; there may be lots of them, and I hope to take some training next year to help decipher them. But how many are there? Are there any other possibilities? I called my old friend in Western Missouri and posed the same question to him. He said that the same thing had bothered him some years ago, although he too believes in the signs and has followed many in Missouri, Arkansas, Oklahoma, and some other states. Here is an edited version of some notes he sent me.—Steve.

"I have sought KGC sites and done research for over 30 years. I work primarily in southern Missouri, Arkansas, and Oklahoma, but have been to both coasts in this pursuit. I have been slightly successful, but still am waiting for the Big One. Since I have retired, I am now in this full time.

When the first surveys were done before the Civil War in the 1830s, they primarily blazed trees, carved on trees and rocks, and only sometimes actually took time to erect a monument. When the good survey came in the 1880s, they had to try to find all of the older markers. Sometimes this is very difficult.

Not only were there surveys by the US land office, sometimes through several generations, but some areas have Spanish and even French surveys as well. The US surveys followed the ordinance of 1785, subdividing land west of the Appalachian Mountains into townships and sections. In Arkansas, for example, it was a portion of French Louisiana, which was transferred to the Spanish in 1763, back to the French in 1801 and sold to the US in 1803.

There were also Spanish land grants dating primarily from 1791 to

1797. Each corner was carved with the initials of the owner and various other descriptive data with an iron carver. This was generally done on trees, minimum height of 3 feet, and a mound of dirt was raised around the tree. Other natural features were used if they could sufficiently be located. Trees were blazed along the line of transient and in Texas, a cross was often used rather than a simple blaze.

The first American survey in Arkansas started in 1815 and really just got a good start by 1821. They generally followed the procedures indicated by the US land office back in the 1800s. Corners were often marked with items like pottery, metallic objects, or carved stones onto the dirt pile near the corner. At any rate, these markings often contained numbers relating to distances and bearings and the dedication number, and sometimes initials of the property owner, or surveyor.

It is my theory that at least some of these have been mistaken for KGC signs and may have misled some treasure hunters. It is also quite possible that some older, existing, survey signs may have been modified by the KGC for their own purposes or used for some of their burial sites.

I am NOT trying to discredit KGC signs, just to provide some data to separate true from untrue signs."

Chapter Five

Newsletters From May 1998 To October 2001

TO KGC, OR NOT TO KGC? By Steve Ryland
May 1998, Volume 14, Number Five

In the past month we have received letters regarding the KGC that are rather different in their viewpoints. Since we have mention the KGC so many times, I thought we might open a little more light on this topic and open a discussion.

I think everyone must agree that there WAS a Knights of the Golden Circle. There were cells among the Copperheads in the Midwest and around many of the mining camps throughout the West. The movement was also, along with numerous other groups, common among the southern partisans in the Western Frontier of the Civil War. Both Roy and I have some family ties to what may have had some relation to the KGC--he in Kansas and Oklahoma, and I in Missouri.

To most of the treasure hunting fraternity there is known to be a group of very avid KGC investigators who have sought, sometimes successfully, KGC treasures throughout the West and Southern Midwest. The more radical of these consider the KGC as almost the source of all treasure, either directly, or as the ultimate treasure hunters, who have found and reburied nearly all U.S. terrestrial treasures ranging from Beale (a little early) to the Lost Dutchman to Victoria Peak, and many others. KGC signs and codes can thus lead us to most all troves. Further, the KGC financed the aviation industry, WWI, etc (See "Jesse James Was One of His Names" by Del Schrader.)

It is obvious that the truth lies somewhere in between, as with most things in life. The following is a letter from one of our subscribers. Note, that there is discussion of the Masons and, not being a Mason, I can neither confirm nor deny the author's premises. –Steve.

The Letter

"I have been a THC subscriber nearly from the beginning with Larry. Thank you for keeping it going. In some ways I liked Larry better, but you are different and sometimes better in other ways.

"We have not had too many articles on the KGC lately and I thought I would throw this at you along my line of research. Most think the KGC is related to people like Quantrill and Jesse James, and was a movement to rebuild the south after the Civil War, maybe centered in Arkansas and Texas rather than in the southeast. This could have been one aspect to the activity of the KGC, but this was just a small branch on the tree of the KGC, which had much older and widespread origins.

"The true KGC is a sect of Freemasons. Masonry came to America from England and Scotland in the early 1700s, just as formal societies were being established over there. Many of the founding fathers of the U.S. were Masons, particularly Benjamin Franklin. As you can see from the design of the Seal, as seen on the dollar bill, there are a number of Masonic influences. British Masonry was adopted among the wealthy class and the grandmaster for much of its history was a prince of royal blood. Also, in the U.S., the more prominent men became Masons, or at least friendly with them. This included many politicians and industrialists in the north as well as southern aristocrats, particularly in Virginia.

"Later, an alternate Freemason group was founded in Charleston, South Carolina with ties more to continental Europe than to England. It found its strength more in the heart of the south and to the west; its membership was commonly not so exalted as the earlier groups and had more popular support.

"During the Civil War, at the beginning, much of Europe supported the South, maybe promoted by wanting cotton and other goods. Later, through manipulation by financial interests and European financiers such as the Rothschilds, not to mention the southern decline in fortunes after the Battle of Gettysburg, the support was abandoned.

"During this time was forged the great Anglo-American economic interweave which has ever since dominated our international outlook. These connections are not only financial, but a little religious and probably represent by far the most powerful of any good-old-boy group that has ever been. This association is full of secret and not-so-secret societies including the Bilderbergers, the TriLateral Commission, the Council on Foreign Affairs, the New World Order, and others. Most of our presidents and cabinet officers, and a large number of politicians have either been members or friends with some of these groups.

"What happened to the poor boys in Dixie when this alliance was struck? Well, it seems to me that to many mainstream southern leaders, that it was a break in a sworn affiliation, even more powerful than a declaration of war. After many years and new generations, in the new south, this has mended itself to some extent.

"However, to the southerners on the frontier, in the western states, this was a full affront to everything they held faithfully. This caused them to break with the existing South Carolina group, from other groups, and to avoid the carpetbagger spies, they formed primarily secret groups. Not unrelated to the KGC, was the original KKK, Knights of the White Camellia, etc. Later, these groups changed their emphasis into the 20th century.

"My research indicates the KGC was not just a group of disgruntled people here and there, but a unified force with sworn loyalty based on their earlier Masonic framework. They recovered wealth from their associates in the western mines, they robbed banks and railroads as almost a guerilla activity, they broke from the current politicians, the financial institutions, and the Jews. They invested wisely but independently and were among the first speculative venture capitalists for western growth and development. They financed some of the early automotive, aircraft, and petroleum industries. They did generate great wealth.

"In order to preserve some of this wealth for future generations, they did hide it in complex depositories, primarily in the southwestern redoubt (an arc from Kentucky and Tennessee, through Arkansas and Texas, into Arizona). Among the members were skilled surveyors and scholars. Most of these depositories are based on the Masonic geometries, on secrets from the Knights Templar, and were actualized by highly skilled workers.

"As treasure hunters, this is a major line of research. I think that some of these treasures are meant to be found by those smart enough to find them and to camouflage the greater treasures. I know this to be controversial, but I also think that the KGC still does exist, perhaps in some different form, and may yet protect some of those secrets and treasures. .

"I am not a practicing Mason of any type, although I had a minimum involvement in a lodge before Korea. I cannot guarantee all of this information, but the pieces just keep stringing themselves together. I will let you know my progress in these matters." AM-Birmingham, AL

(Well, I hope some of you do know more about these things, certainly I don't know much myself. I am sure we have a number of Masons as subscribers. Does this theory make any sense at all? Are there some truths? At any rate, we are soliciting further discussion of the KGC and related matters. Send us a letter or Email—Steve Ryland.)

JESSE JAMES REMAINS MYSTERIOUS

From The Daily Oklahoman, September 4, 1995

June 1998, Volume 14, Number 6

Encased in glass and laid carefully inside a purple cloth bag is one of Michael Griffith's most prized possessions.

A man's image graces the front of the yellowed, obviously old cardboard. But the costly card doesn't feature a professional baseball player or even an autographed picture of a movie star. It's the final picture of Jesse Woodson James, his eyes closed and hands folded in death. Or is it?

"As spectacular a story as all this is, it just doesn't add up." said Griffith, a history teacher and coach in the Choctaw-Nicoma Park School District.

Griffith can't deny the value of the "cabinet card," used to identify the dead awaiting burial at the undertakers in the late 1800's. But he also can't deny that the corpse laid out so neatly in suit and tie could be Charlie Biggelow, a former James' crony who looked so much like James that many people couldn't tell them apart.

Add to the mix, the fabled death scene (legend has it that James was shot in the back by former friends, the Ford brothers, while straightening a sampler on the wall.) Throw in the desperado's love of hoaxes (many believe James faked his death to escape certain death or prison exile). And factor in the reality that James was photographed rarely (only 13 verified pictures of the infamous outlaw exist.)

The result: Serious doubt as to whether or not the individual buried in the

Kearney, MO., grave six feet under James' tombstone is, indeed, Jesse James.

Experts at George Washington University's National Center for Forensic Science, hope to answer that question this month. The remains believed for so long to be James' were exhumed July 31 and have been scrutinized ever since.

A report on the findings, including DNA testing aided by blood relatives, will be made public September 22, and a comprehensive scientific report will be issued February 22, said professor Jim Starrs.

Griffith is eagerly awaiting those results. Perhaps more so than the third and fourth generation descendants of the Old West's most elusive bandit.

The amateur historian has immersed himself in post-Civil War history for the past six years. His studies have led him on a trail of intrigue--and even treasure hunting--that sometimes keeps him awake at night with unanswered questions and fragments of information.

Griffith believes Jesse James, his brother, Frank James, and the Ford brothers faked the outlaw's death after the Missouri governor put a $10,000 bounty on Jesse James' head. Griffith said a paper trail scattered across America and signed by J. Frank Dalton (commonly known to be Jesse James' alias, an orderly combination of his first initial, brother's first name and mother's maiden name)--lends credence to this theory, Griffith said.

"And then there's the fact that his brother went into business with the Fords later." Griffith said. "Not a common thing to do with the people that murdered your brother."

The history buff's love for all things related to James has brought financial gain, as well. In December 1993, Griffith said he and two others decoded one of Frank and Jesse James' maps and unearthed a Wells Fargo safe full of gold coins. He won't say where because other excavations are planned near there.

"I could talk for days about what I've learned and what I plan to do in the future to find out more," Griffith said. "I've never seen anything so complicated in my life."

FOUND! JESSE JAMES' $2 MILLION KEECHI HILLS GOLD HORD

June 1998, Volume 14, Number 6, by Bob Brewer

For those of you who still doubt the existence of the CONFEDERATE UNDERGROUND and their millions in buried Rebel treasure, this is a true story about the actual recovery of a well known treasure that was searched for by treasure hunters for almost century. Long said to be a Jesse James cache, this treasure indeed was originally buried by old Jesse, but was consolidated with other wealth and placed into a KGC depository in 1889. Like I said before, the story is true, but the names used here are fictitious to protect the identities of the innocent and the guilty.

First, just in case you are not familiar with the KNIGHTS, let me run this by you!

There are rumors which have persisted for over a hundred years, claiming that a secret Confederate organization known as the KGC, robbed and pillaged Yankee owned banks, railroads, etc. for over fifty years after the cessation of open hostilities between the North and South. Using Quantrill-type tactics, this underground Rebel Army robbed, embezzled, and diverted millions in Yankee gold, silver, and greenback dollars and stashed the riches away in secret underground depositories for use later to finance a second War of Rebellion.

Around 1973, a seemingly ridiculous book was published that stated the KGC and KKK were organizations composed of soldiers belonging to a super secret underground Confederate Army. This book further claimed that Jesse James and his band of brigands were in reality soldiers of that Rebel Underground Army.

After years of research and investigation, proof can be presented that this group of old Confederates did exist and that they did indeed bury treasure.

To introduce this exciting new evidence, let me explain that a group calling itself GOLDEN CIRCLE RESEARCH, for obvious reasons, is privileged with certain information that may not be available to other people or groups.

Recently, news arrived, via the treasure hunter's grapevine, that a very large Rebel treasure depository was discovered in the Southwest. This depository contained six very large caches of gold and silver bullion, boxes of gold and silver coins, and an unknown amount of jewelry. The precise location of this mass of treasure was not disclosed to this writer, but evidence was presented during a confidential interview, by a treasure hunter who claims he recovered a very large cache of this Rebel gold, that leaves no doubt as to the truth of the matter.

During this audio taped meeting, the treasure hunter displayed some of the gold coins from the cache including a new ring made from a $5.00 quarter eagle coin. Also shown were photos of treasure and an inventory sheet listing gold coins by denomination and number. The treasure hunter admitted he had two partners in the treasure search, but declined to name them.

Later, by burning up the phone lines, the identity of those two partners was learned by a process of elimination. It also was learned that the lucky treasure hunter had not informed his partners of any recovery, nor had he shared the proceeds as required by their partnership agreement.

One of those partners agreed to an interview providing his identity be kept confidential. The following story he told without stuttering or batting an eye. Quoted verbatim:……

THE STORY

"The modern search for this treasure began over 63 years ago, when an old treasure hunter named Joe Hunter, who was active in the 1930's and 1940's, discovered a cache of gold and jewelry buried in a cast iron tea kettle near Buzzard's Roost, a well known landmark in southwestern Oklahoma. This discovery was reported by the Lawton Constitution, a Lawton Oklahoma newspaper, in 1948. However, the article neglected to mention some of the kettle's contents. Besides the gold and jewelry buried in the kettle were several (?) at least two or three maps. These maps were carved on thin copper sheet metal, rolled into a tube, and placed in the kettle.

Of course, after finding the maps, Joe Hunter searched for the treasure locations, but to no avail. The maps were cryptic using a mysterious cipher, which Hunter or no one else seemed to be able to break.

After Hunter's death, the maps eventually found their way into the hands of Ed, a noted researcher/historian, well versed in western history. Ed knew the maps were valuable, but had no idea of how to decipher them, so he permitted his friend Bill (the lucky treasure hunter) to make a copy of the maps. The two partners agreed to divide equally anything found with Ed's maps.

Unable to do anything with the ciphered maps himself, Bill showed them to one treasure hunter after another trying to break the ciphers, but had no luck. Finally he sought the help of an old professional treasure hunter named Dick, who had a reputation for being able to read outlaw and pirate treasure maps.

After seeing the waybills or maps, Dick agreed to decipher them and tell Bill where the treasure was buried for half of the cache. Bill was elated when in a few months Dick finally deciphered the maps, and being an honest man told him the treasure's location.

The irony of this story is that Ed, who had supplied the maps, and Dick, the map-reader, were acquainted and soon discovered that Bill, the middle man, was playing both ends against the middle. Bill failed to mention to his partner, Ed, that he now knew the location of the treasure, and he kept giving Dick flimsy excuses about why he had not tried to get permission to enter the property where the treasure was buried.

Dick, the treasure hunter who deciphered the maps, had insisted that Bill obtain a recovery contract from the landowner before they attempted a recovery of any of the six caches. Bill by now, eaten up with the "greeds," figured out how he could have all the treasure to himself. Without obtaining permission, he illegally entered the property where one of the treasure caches was buried and dug up a Wells Fargo box of gold coins, the majority being $20.00 gold pieces. The exact amount of the find is not known, but the map, which leads to the cache, indicated the treasure was $200,000 in gold coins (face value). At today's gold prices, without considering the numismatic worth of gold coins, the treasure would be worth a staggering $3,500,000 to $4,000,000 dollars. Depending on the rarity of the coins and their denominations, that figure could easily double or triple! Not a bad haul for a rank amateur!

Naturally, now that Bill had all of this gold in his possession, he would forget to inform his partners of the find. However, Bill is a blabbermouth and wants everyone to know that he is a big time treasure hunter. Soon, word spread among treasure hunters that he had made a big strike! In the meantime, Dick suspecting Bill was up to something contacted Ed to see what their buddy was doing, and discovered that the maps actually belonged to Ed, not Bill.

Ed and Dick then joined forces to find out where Bill had gotten his treasure. They visited the ranch where Dick suspected Bill had recovered one of the caches from Ed's map. They informed the landowner of their suspicions and a quick check was made where a chest of gold should have been buried. Sure enough, at the exact spot indicated on the map, they found a smoking hole dug only days before and left open. (For you not in the know, a well-restored recovery site makes it impossible to tell where something was removed and therefore, there is no evidence left. Open holes are the sure sign of an amateur's work.)

Dick explained to the property owner how the crime was perpetrated, who the culprit was, and he and Ed offered to provide evidence to aid in the prosecution of Bill. Dick also took the time to visit the other five treasure sites and removed or hid the clues needed to locate those treasures. Now, even the maps are useless!

It's now understood that the landowner has started legal proceedings to have Bill arrested and prosecuted. He and his accomplices will be charged with criminal trespass and grand theft. The case is being built with the help of Ed, the researcher who originally had possession of the maps, and Dick, who deciphered the maps.

Ed tells us that the most amazing thing in this whole story is that Bill has practically convicted himself with letters and documents he mailed to his partner, Dick. One letter describes how Bill and his father had to park and walk over a mile to sneak into the property to search for the treasure. Another strange, quirk is that a witness has been located that saw the thief, and two or three others with him at the scene of the crime on a day last summer.

Ed laughs. What will be the most shocking thing for the dishonest treasure hunter to find out is that he was set up. Dick, the old Pro, had dealt with Bill's type many times before. Bill was given the direction to only one cache, the smallest! The other five fabulous caches, one of which, we are told contains about 3,200 pounds of gold, lay untouched with only Dick knowing their location. The landowner has posted armed guards on his property to prevent further trespassing and has given Ed and Dick permission to begin recovery operations as soon as the legal proceedings against Bill are complete.

For obvious reasons, Ed, who provided Golden Circle Research with this information, wishes to remain anonymous, but told us he has seen Rebel documents that indicate there were three maps to this treasure depository. When we asked Ed to let us view the maps, he declined, saying they were in storage. He did, however, tell us where one of the maps used to locate this treasure could be found. The map was printed in a treasure book years ago, entitled "Oklahoma

Treasures and Treasure Trails." The map is a site map giving specific directions and distances for only two of the caches and is totally useless if the exact location of the depository is not known. Ed confided that this depository is actually the treasure known as JESSE JAMES' $2,000,000 KEECHI HILLS TREASURE or THE BURRO SHOE TREASURE, and has been written up in numerous treasure slicks.

Our final question to Ed was: "Where in heaven's name is this place?" Ed just smiled, shook our hand, and pointed west as he silently left the motel where the interview took place.

READERS ROUNDTABLE

June 1998, Volume 14, Number 6

You will remember last month that we had some articles regarding the Knights of the Golden Circle. They have spawned a variety of reactions and here are a few:

Researcher-Arkansas- We have proof of large scale KGC operations. There are still those alive who overlap and have tales from KGC members and their descendents. Based on our investigations of the complex KGC depositories, it is possible that there was a strong Masonic component although I don't think calling the KGC a sect of the Masons is proper.

Researcher-California - I was interested to see a small reference to the Anti-Semitism of the KGC in one of the letters. Most KGC members that I have researched were fundamentalists. However, the highest officials had a more complex, hidden religion. Although this is only hinted at in documents, it may be related to British Israelism (Identity Movement) indicating that the Chosen are in fact not the Jews but certain people of British extraction. This could also support some kind of Masonic connection.

Researcher-Kansas -Based on my studies of some KGC members, they traveled far and wide throughout the United States and overseas. This does not seem appropriate for "backwoods" people from the South. For instance, we know of Jesse James's trips to California. This was done in a time, except for the war, when most people did not travel over 30 miles from their birthplace throughout their lifetime. I do think there is a connection, perhaps with the

Masons, or perhaps with something else.

(We are soliciting further discussion of the KGC and related matters. Send us a letter or Email-Steve)

KGC TREASURE CAVERN FOUND

June 1998, Volume 14, Number 6

Gene Ballinger, Editor of the "The Institute News Magazine," received a phone call to say that a major depository had been discovered with a portion of the Confederate Treasury, all sorts of other artifacts, and Confederate documents. There were no markings or signs, and it was on private ranch property. Some of the treasure hunters may have been from Louisiana. There is a picture in the article which certainly looks like a Western sandstone bluff.

DISCUSSION WITH MIKE WALSH ON THE KGC

May 2000, Volume 16, Number 4

I've had a discussion with THC friend Mike Walsh of Osceola, Missouri. You may remember that Mike was skeptical about some of the so-called KGC inscriptions in the Ozarks, and attributed many of them to old surveyor markings. Now Mike, at my urging, is preparing an article on "KGC Connections and Coincidences."

Just to give you a teaser, Mike has pretty good proof that the key figure of the KGC was General Albert Pike. He was a mason and closely related to the Knights Templar and the CSA. The KGC (and by the way, the KKK) were not founded by Pike, but his philosophy heavily influenced both of them and he later rather co-opted both groups for his ends.

Thus, Mike feels that the KGC is a direct lineal descendent of the Knights Templar (no longer Catholic, of course) and that the KGC treasures are more than simple, Civil War stashes and may represent a thousand years of accumulation. He also argues that many of those well known as KGC researchers are far more than that.

At any rate, we hope to have this next month. Now, if Mike is on the right track,......Well, I have suggested he watch his back.

THE TRUTH ABOUT THE KGC, By Mike Walsh

June 2000, Volume 16, Number 6

Just a word about me. I live in a little town in west-central Missouri. I have lived in the area for most of my life and my family has been here since the 1840s. I am a history buff and interested in, but not avid with, treasure hunting. I have always been a little skeptical about all the stories of the James boys and the KGC treasures and markers, but know some of the stories to be true.

Steve (Ryland) has been after me to write on this topic. I have known Steve since we were kids when he returned to Missouri from Pinar Del Rio back in 1959. Our parents knew each other before the War.

At any rate, I will give a 2-3 part story on this, not 20-plus parts like some around here. Let me know if you have any comments. By the way, even though it may seem differently, I have nothing against the Masons; some of my best friends are Masons.

THE ORIGINS OF THE KNIGHTS OF THE GOLDEN CIRCLE

When most of us hear about the KGC, we think of Confederate allies in the north ("Copperheads") or small expatriate groups in the goldfields of California and many other western states. Some think that the KGC was a "club" like the Knights of the White Camellia or the KKK, formed toward the end or after the Civil War. While all these are partly true, it is much more, and maybe very much more. I will provide some facts with bibliography, and also some speculation.

The Knights of the Golden Circle had its origin long before the Civil War. It is definitely and clearly traced to George Bickley no later than 1854. Bickley was from Virginia, but founded the KGC in Cincinnati, Ohio. It had chapters, called "castles," ranging from New York to California.

Its principal purpose was to annex all or part of Mexico. Bickley left Ohio and found a great deal of support in Texas, and the group may have even included Sam Houston. They tried to mount at least two expeditions across the Rio Grande in around 1860, but both met with complete failure. He was later arrested as a confederate spy in Indiana and died in 1865. There was interaction with the Copperhead movement in the North. This aspect of the KGC fades away after 1867.

However, there is a much grander origin of the KGC, not as well documented, but perhaps closer to the truth. As early as 1800, there were filibusterers who sought to invade adjacent foreign territory in Spanish, and later independent, Mexico. These included Aaron Burr and John Wilkerson. Some of these folks later participated in the War of Texas Independence and the Mexican War. As you might imagine, there were a number who wanted to go further, to expand the Texas Republic into Mexico. Others, such as some members of the Kearny and Doniphan expeditions in the Mexican War, also were interested in significant occupation and territorial incorporation. The seeds of the KGC were being sown and many of the later officials started in these eras. Albert Pike was roaming Texas and New Mexico in those days,

When the Mexican War drew to a close, General John Quitman became military governor of Mexico City. He provided a plan to president Polk for the annexation of most of Mexico into the U.S. as slave territory. In 1850 he became governor of Mississippi and called a secession convention in Nashville. There, he proposed a privately sponsored invasion of Mexico. This caused his indictment under the neutrality act; some say President Zachary Taylor was poisoned by the group. Quitman, along with Jefferson Davis and Caleb Cushing (who had opened China to trade), got Franklin Pierce elected, partly financed by British money.

Now, for a bit more murky, conspiracy theory aspect. In turns out that all of the characters we have, mentioned, as well as many more, were all Scottish Rite Masons and much of the financing came from Britain through the Rothschild family of bankers. Quitman had become a Mason in 1830 and was made Sovereign Grand Inquisitor General after the Mexican War. Many consider the KGC to have been a Masonic terrorist underground and used Masonic signs, grips, and passwords.

In 1853, Quitman, along with Slidell, Benjamin, Davis (all later CSA guys), with British financing, recruited up to 50,000 volunteers to invade Cuba and then Mexico and Central America to form a vast Caribbean-based slave empire. When the initial force (ship Black Warrior) was captured by the Spanish in Havana, this phase of activity was curtailed. In addition to Bickley, Killian Van Rensselaer and the Quitman group founded the KGC. This group was more extreme and had in mind to exterminate the Catholic Hispanics and replace them with more slaves from Africa.

Quitman died in 1859, which brings us to Albert Pike. Albert Pike had roamed Texas and New Mexico as a youth. He had not even heard of the Masons until 1853. Then he was sponsored and became a political boss in Arkansas. He joined the supreme council in 1859 along with John Breckenridge, democratic presidential candidate in 1860. He is said to have co-written the Confederate Constitution in 1861.

The conspiracy theory continues in that much of the Civil War was financed by British and French loans with all sorts of Masonic connections between CSA officials, such as Benjamin Judah, John Slidell, and James Bullock, all former KGC operatives, Further, this promoted the French invasion of Mexico as a step in the KGC plan.

For some reason, many Native Americans became active in the Masons and also the KGC, and it is well documented among the Cherokees and Chickasaws in Oklahoma and the Sioux in Minnesota. Well known are the Cherokee "Blue Lodges" which transformed themselves into KGC "castles." By the way, Albert Pike was Confederate Indian Commissioner. Although there was considerable espionage and sabotage in the North, and even with foreign financing, the Southern Cause was lost. Although there are rumors, it is probably unfounded that John Wilkes Booth was a member of the KGC. Many of the people we have discussed moved permanently to Europe.

During reconstruction, we are all aware of the founding of the Ku Klux Klan in Nashville, Tennessee in 1867 by Nathan Bedford Forrest, and Albert Pike. The KKK of 1867, of course, was rather different than its reincarnations of 1915 and 1960s. It is a direct outgrowth of the KGC, formed primarily by masons, and even kept part of the name "kyklos"=ku klux--Greek for Circle.

In 1865, Pike fled to Britain. However, under pressure from the Masons to the Masonic president Andrew Johnson, Pike was allowed to return in 1866. Pike granted Johnson Masonic degrees 4-32; some say this later was a factor in his impeachment. Pike moved to Tennessee. He was said to have been appointed as chief judicial officer of the KKK, although this is either not well documented, or covered-up.

Although president Grant hated the KKK, he also fought long and hard for the annexation of Cuba, a KGC goal. Pike later moved the Southern Masonic Scottish Rite temple To Washington, D.C.

This conspiracy stuff gets even weirder. Teddy Roosevelt, who finally helped to conquer Cuba, became president. He was an admirer of Pike and, by the way, nephew of Bullock, one of the pre-war KGC officials. Franklin Pierce's direct descendent is Barbara Pierce Bush, wife of George Bush and father of GW. Makes you have a different idea of international bankers and that whole thing, doesn't it? Well, look for yourself.

Next time, we will go back to Albert Pike, how the KGC may have acquired Spanish treasure, and then the more speculative Knights Templar/Masons/Pike/KGC connection.

KGC BIBLIOGRAPHY—THOUGHT NOT COMPLETE
(Here, you can read about the KGC yourself)

June 2000, Volume 16, Number 6

Ager, W.I., 1947, The Great Northwestern Conspiracy.

Atlantic Monthly. 1880, The Chicago Conspiracy, v 16, p 108-120. Allsop, F. W., 1920, The Life of Albert Pike. Little Rock.
Buice, S., 1970, The Civil War and the Five Civilized Tribes, Ph.D Dissertation, University of Oklahoma.

Chronicles of Oklahoma, 1953, Confederate Government Relations with the
Five Civilized Tribes, v 31, p 189-204.

Crenshaw, 0:, 1941, The Knights of the Golden Circle: The Career of George Bickley, American Historical Review, v 47, October, 1941.

Duncan, R., 1961, Reluctant General: The Life and Times of Albert Pike. New York.

Dunn, R.S., 1967, The KGC in Texas, Southwestern Historical Quarterly, v

70, April, 1967.

Feeler, M., 1902, Secret Political Societies in the North during the Civil War

Hicks, J., 1961, Some Letters Concerning the Knights of the Golden Circle, Southwestern Historical Quarterly, v 65, July, 1961.

Indiana Magazine of History, 1965, Carrington and the Golden Circle Legend in Indiana During the Civil War, v 61.

May, R.E.,1973, The Southern Dream of a Caribbean Empire. 1854-1861, LSU Press.

Milton, G.F., Abraham Lincoln and the Fifth Column.

Pike, A., 1861, Message of the President and Report of Albert Pike. Commissioner of the Confederate State to the Indian Nations West of Arkansas. Richmond.

Pike, A, 1882, Morals and Dogma.

Ryland, S.L., 1970, The Jews, the Cherokees, and the Southern Expansion to the West, Southern Partisan, v 2, p 88-93.

Shrader, Del, 1972, Jesse James was One of his Names, Arcadia, CA.

Stidger, F.G., 1865, The Treason History of the Order of Sons of Liberty. Formerly Circle of Honor, Succeeded by Knights of the Golden Circle: The Most Gigantic Treasonable Conspiracy the World Has Ever Known.—(This was reprinted a few years ago.)

Texas State Historical Society, 1999, Handbook of Texas Online, http://www.tsha.utexas.edu

EDITORIAL -- WHAT HAPPENED TO THC????
By Steve Ryland.

August-October 2000, Volume 16, Number 8

It was late in the afternoon on August 25th. It was hot in Southern California, over 105°. I was sitting in my office in Pasadena with the air conditioners at full blast. Suddenly, three men entered the office. They said they were treasure hunters and by their accent (much like mine) I knew they were native to the lower Midwest, maybe Oklahoma, or Arkansas. They wanted to know if I wanted to participate with them on a hunt in Texas. Of course, I said I would, being always ready to go.

They apparently knew me from the THC and talked about how they liked it; I thanked them modestly. Then the leader of the three directly asked, "Do you know anything about the Knights of the Golden Circle?" I indicated that I have studied them, perhaps had had some relatives involved in the distant past, and that we incidentally had been running a series on them to the THC.

He responded, "Do you mean the articles by Mike Walsh of Missouri?" I affirmed his observation, but then started to become a bit nervous. Mike had called a couple of times and indicated that he had gotten a lot of e-mail on the articles and was questioned as to what would be in the final installment about the KGC today. In fact, he had people visit him at his home, and he was a little excited about the whole thing.

Another of the men asked if I thought the KGC was still alive today. I said something like there are probably some descendents around and maybe someone knows where some other caches might be. He followed up his question with a comment something like, "Based on Mike Walsh's article, he seems to think that there is more to the KGC than a simple bunch of ex- Confederates. What you think?" I indicated that I had an open mind on the subject and there was certainly some evidence to that effect.

"Mr. Ryland," the leader asserted. "You know in this life, there are just some things that everyone doesn't need to know about. I think your little articles on the KGC were great, but you know, enough is enough! Do you have Walsh's last article?"

I replied that I did not and was waiting for it. One of the others joked,
"I think you may wait awhile." No more was said of the treasure hunt nor

anything else and the three men left, saying they just might have to visit me again some day.

I immediately called Mike Walsh in Missouri. There was no answer then, nor has there been for the past three months. Letters have been returned.

I hope you understand why the THC has been delayed for a time.

THE REAL KGC-CONCLUSION, by Mike Walsh

January-September 2001, Volume 17, Number 1

NOTE: Remember, two issues ago—Steve mentioned the threats to the News Letter and to me. Well, I have moved, but it had nothing to do with threats-(or so he claims). I just moved into a new rural home, but still in the Missouri…. (and it may be better for his health there, also.)

Well, we have talked about the background of the KGC, and how it may be much more than it seemed at first, much older, and may have been a significant force in politics in the United States. But, what of its position today?

Around 1930, the last of the Confederate veterans were dying off and the various caches were left to a few Watchers--relatives of the original group. Now, something happened at this time, and I still cannot pin it down. There was a great schism within the KGC. Some of my ideas are:

"Simple change of guard between the old and young. Youngsters wanted to "borrow" and use some of the money for personal or other purposes.

"The KKK, which we have seen had great ties to at least some factions of the KGC, was resurgent from 1915 to nearly 1930. Maybe some factions wanted to use the funds to assist the KKK, and maybe they did.

"The more national Masonic faction of the KGC wanted to use, or hold, the funds for future purposes. These purposes could have been largely business related, or be the source of KGC power today--see below.

"Several of these may have been influenced by the stock market crash and depression. This may also, in some sort of conspiratorial way, have been tied to gaining political and financial power."

At any rate, during this time, many of the depositories were recovered, inventoried, and re-hidden. I tend to think the answer may be closest to the third proposal above. This is the time that the Masonic faction pushed what we might call the Confederate faction out of control and power. Sure, there are a number of pre-1930 caches still around and that is what is typically found by our research.

There are today, Watchers, (or Sentinels) who keep an eye on these areas and discourage any exploration, by the great and great-great, and more remote grandsons of the Confederacy. I have met those who say that they are these, who I tend not to believe, and those who you just rather know really are, primarily in the Southern Midwest.

I fear the vast majority of the wealth, knowledge, and power are now in somewhat different hands--this wealth is in banks worldwide, in the stock markets, and in the coffers of the Fortune 500.

We have seen that there is a strong alliance between the KGC and the Masons and other secret societies in Ivy League universities and some Western groups as well. By the very nature of the memberships of these groups, there is an interlocking realm of common commitment, goals, and an envisionment for the progress of the U.S., both politically and in business. Now, I don't want to go on any kind of right-wing rant regarding Bilderburgers, Tri-Lateralists, etc. but these too have similar intermeshing memberships which have included several of the recent presidents as well as much of Congress and other people of authority in government and business. Now, this sort of geo-political "conspiracy" is probably not an organized--you do that--we do this, etc, plan, but just a common purpose of those in the group.

This a long way from what our general idea of the KGC of old was, and a very long way from its secondary origins among Confederate veterans, but I think that the true power base of the KGC is now that of the ruling class in the U.S. and by extension much of the World.

P.S. I recently heard of a correlation between a Mexican treasure in Southern Texas with the KGC and the Knights Templar. Sometimes these things are hard to believe, but they keep showing up.

Chapter Six

Is The Famous LUE Treasure Part of The KGC Treasure?

By Roy Roush

Some of you might not have heard of the famous LUE treasure and its mysterious map since little is known about it even today, although it has been around for more than 30 years, it's still an enigma. During my research on the subject many years ago when I was writing the "Q&A Department" for TREASURE MAGAZINE, I found out that its name was coined from the first letters of the words: "Lloro, Urraca and Enterrari." Look those words up and it may give you some clues on the treasure. It's also sometimes known as the LEAUX treasure.

There's all kinds of speculation about the treasure. Some of the old thinking at first was that it was a key to Spanish treasure. Then later, others seemed to believe that it was a key to a huge treasure of gold bullion buried in this country by the Nazis before World War II to somehow help finance their efforts during the war. Others seemed to believe that it is a key to the Mexican National's 17 tons of gold bullion that was brought into this country in about 1930 and buried, probably in New Mexico, in hopes of selling it to the US mint later; but failing to do that, it still lies buried somewhere. (I have searched for that one myself several times.)

But when treasure hunters began to learn about the KGC and their manner of doing things a few years back, many now believe that it could be part of the KGC treasure--and I might agree with that.

KARL Von MUELLER

To my knowledge, the old treasure hunter and prolific writer, Karl von Mueller (whose real name was Dean Miller) was the first to write about it. The map first appeared in 1972 in his "Treasure Hunters Manual, Number Seven." Karl was basically known for his "Treasure Hunter's Manuals" written during the 1960's and 1970's. They are classics today.

His comments about it were that it would perplex treasure hunters for years to come. He said that only two people had ever been able to decipher it, and they would never be able to carry away all of the incredible treasures that are revealed by the map. He added that others would look for it, but only a few would succeed, and they would be committed to eternal secrecy when they learned the cryptic and shibboleth hoard of all hordes on the American continent. He also said that true sign experts will find the ultimate in challenges in this key to a natural Fort Knox.

His information on it was not in any of his previous writings, nor in any other publications before that that I know of. I'm sure that it was one of his pet projects that he had largely been keeping to himself (which is typical for most treasure hunters.) But by this time, Karl was suffering from heart problems and he knew that his time was limited--maybe that's why he revealed it in his last publication.

I knew Karl very well. We also exchanged letters for years. We both had been technical writers for some aerospace companies in Los Angeles for a number of years. He was an old-time treasure Hunter--actually being among the first to dedicate a lot of time and effort in the field-- often with good results. And being a prolific writer, he wrote many books and articles on the subject-- more than anybody else at the time, and is responsible for converting more people to treasure hunting than anyone else I know. For me, he re-ignited my longtime interest in the subject, and I also became very active in the field.

Karl never gave me much real information on the LUE treasure, except to say how great the treasure was. He said it was the biggest buried treasure in the United States, and that he thought that it was located in the southwestern part of the United States--possibly in northern New Mexico somewhere. This could explain why he moved from the Los Angeles area in the early 1960's to a little, old (and mostly ghost town) of Segundo, Colorado, which is located very close to the northern border of New Mexico, in order to search for the treasure.

But some treasure hunters have been concentrating their search in the Rocky Mountains and the southern part of Colorado, especially in the Sangre de Cristo Mountains of Colorado. Also, Karl wrote a book entitled "TREASURE OF THE VALLEY OF SECRETS" under the pen name of Deek Gladsone. I never read the book, but I'm suspicious that he was writing about the LUE treasure. Also, I seem to recall something about a place called "Scarlet Valley" or "The Scarlet Shadow" in relation to the treasure.

Karl was also a good friend of an old-time, hard rock miner and treasure hunter from San Diego who went by the name of Bill "Hardrock" Hammond. Karl had learned much about mining, prospecting, and treasure hunting from the old guy and they often spend much time in the field together. When Hardrock died, Karl wrote an obituary in one of the old treasure publications in about 1972 in which he claimed that Hardrock had actually found some of the LUE treasure.

Whether that was true, or not, I don't know. It could have just been that Karl was exalting his friend with notable achievements. Sometimes, Karl would tell just a little bit more than he really knew.

When Karl hinted to me that he had found some of it, I assumed that they either had found it together, or he had been led there by Hardrock. (It's quite possible that they just stumbled upon it while out on a treasure

The Incredible 'LUE' Treasure Map.......

Map reproduced here from "Treasure Hunter's Manual #7"
Courtesy of the Karl von Mueller Family

hunt for something else, other than being led there by clues.) Karl also said a lot more was still to be found. That would indicate that the LUE treasure is not all at one spot, but spread around to other locations, maybe far apart.

Because the map is so unlike any other treasure maps, some have even thought that Karl made it up just for the sensationalism of it, and maybe also due to his remark that it would keep treasure hunters busy for years trying to figure it out. I wouldn't put something like that past Karl since he did enjoy attention, however I don't think that he did, partly due to his explanation that he had redrawn the map exactly from the "IAY-AYAM KEY."....Whatever that means? Also, there is some evidence now that seems to be coming from other directions.

So, why am I mentioning the LUE treasure? Well, because back then hardly anybody, and probably including Karl, did not know about the treasures of the Knights of the Golden Circle, and therefore no connection was made--until much later when treasure hunters begin to learn about them. If Karl had known about the treasures of the Knights of the Golden Circle, I'm sure he would have written about it, but he did not.

It was pure speculation on the part of some treasure hunters in the past to think that it could have been Spanish, Mexican, or Nazi treasure, since that was before we knew about the treasures of the Knights of the Golden Circle.

Now, if you take a good look at the map, I would say that it certainly does not appear to be associated with anything Spanish or Mexican with anything that I have ever seen before. The old Spanish or Mexican treasure signs and symbols were always rather simple and crude looking. Sometimes, they appeared to be mere Indian petraglyphs, which I'm sure was intentional in order to confuse the wrong people. But the LUE map is far more sophisticated and extremely complex. Nor do I believe that it has anything to do with the Nazis. The most logical explanation is that it was originated by the Knights of the Golden Circle, and most evidence seems to indicate that, since it does fit in with their cryptic and very complex manner of doing things.

Here's a few things that I have heard about the map, and possibly how to decipher it:

THE SYMBOLS ON THE MAP--ARE THEY MASONIC?

The symbols look like they could be from a Masonic source (and I agree.) The all-seeing eye pictured on the American dollar bill is on this map as well as many other symbols. Then look at the very center of the document where the sweeping line comes through the center of the column (which I do not think would be used by Spanish or Mexicans, either). Some think that it means to turn it. Now look just below the center of the column and you will see just two lines coming through the column from the arrow shaft. This also means to turn it. Then you will see that this drawing has two three-dimensional gimbals. Thus, it can spin 360° one-way as well as 360° at 90° in the other direction. ---but I'm not sure that I see it entirely that way.

Then, if you correctly solve the puzzle, you should see that the billion bars are buried under the stair-step pyramid, but where within the pyramid layout is the bullion. That still needs to be figured out.

Some have said that they believe this very large pyramid is within an area about six-by-three miles in size that is outlined by monuments. I assume this means that it is not an upright pyramid, but one outlined horizontally. Otherwise, it would have been found many years ago as a noticeable landmark.

Some have thought that the LUE map is connected to the American one-dollar bill in some way, and that if you look at a dollar bill through a bright light, it will give you a clue, showing that the treasure is under the left leg of the pyramid layout.

This seems rather far-fetched to me, except for some of the resemblance of what appears on the LUE map and also on our one-dollar bill--such as the pyramid and the all-seeing eye. Could that be a coincidence?... Maybe not.

We have pretty much established that the Masons were heavily involved with the Knights of the Golden Circle. And since the Masons were involved in our government and politics, it is thought that some of the symbols shown on the dollar bill are Masonic in origin, and many believe that the Masons received much of their ancient knowledge from the Knights Templar, including their coding system as well. This seems to make pretty good sense to me, and if so, then the cryptic LUE map is a key to some of the Knights of the Golden Circle's treasure. It does seem to have all the earmarks of the KGC.

A LUE MAP OVERLAY

Now, I have some proprietary information on the LUE map that I have in my files that I will present for the benefit of those interested in solving it.

The first is a map overlay that was passed on to me by an old treasure hunter who had been working on it for years when he found out that I was also a serious treasure hunter.

He demonstrated how, that if you could find just one of the treasure locations, you could lay this over a topographical map to locate some of the other sites.

He thought that maybe if we worked on it together, it would lead to a discovery. However, one needs a starting point to begin with, and I was never able to figure that one out. So my intent here is in the hopes that it may be of assistance to you. But remember, if you find something, please send me a little souvenir.

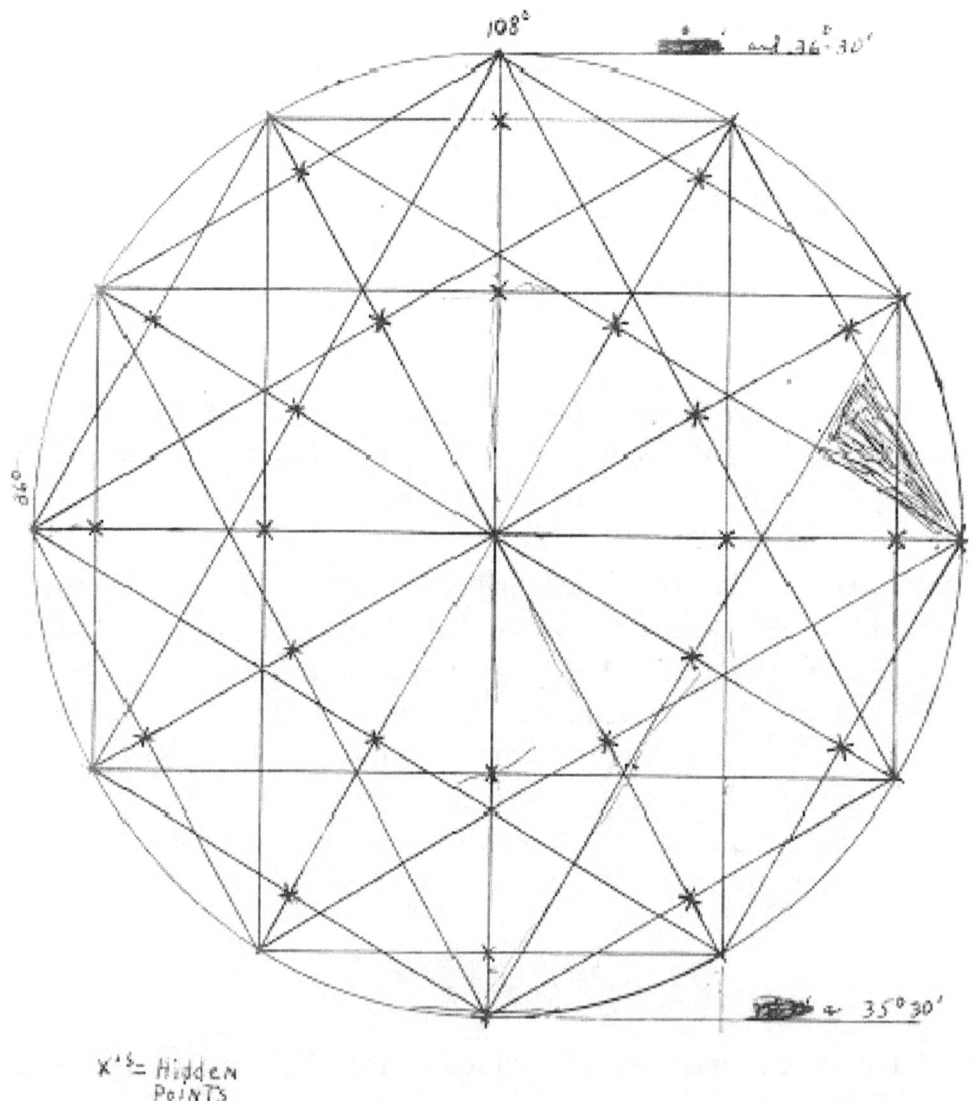

The following is a sketch that he made up of Black Lake Wash in New Mexico, which is just South of Elizabethtown, to show how the overlay could work in a certain area. He used this location because it had been reported somewhere, that two men, just after WWII, had accidentally uncovered two pots of placer gold near there, and he had reason to believe that it was one of the

LUE treasure locations. The gentleman said that he thought he knew pretty close to where some more of the treasure was buried, but he never revealed that to me.

Incidentally, treasure hunters who went looking for treasure around Black Lake, are said to have discovered a series of over 50 holes of varying depth, inclination, and declination, but all were two-inches in diameter. That fits in with the drilled hole at Glorieta Pass, New Mexico I discovered that pointed directly to the spot where some KGC treasure had definitely been buried, but unfortunately, had accidentally been found a few months before.

DEATH TRAPS

One thing though should be kept in mind while searching for KGC treasures--I've heard many warnings of death traps around the treasures to protect them, and I have even seen some of the "warning" indications of death traps posted near some of the sites.

One of those who first told me about the death traps came from my old friend, Bill Mahan from Garland, Texas. He was one of the very earliest of the treasure hunters out there. He was also one of the earliest to manufacture and sell metal detectors back in the 1960's. They were called "D-TEX" detectors. Additionally, he put out one of the finest of all treasure magazines, entitled "TREASURE WORLD." They are real collectors items today.

Bill's experience in treasure hunting went far back before the 1960's. He had searched all along Padre Island in Texas long before it became off-limits to treasure hunting. He had also made many excursions into Mexico and throughout a lot of the United States. He was probably the first to mention the KGC treasures to me, and at the same time, warned me about the dangers. He said that usually it consisted of an explosive charge of either dynamite or black powder; or sometimes it could be a dead-fall, or a water trap in which upon digging to a certain depth, water would suddenly fill up the hole and drown the treasure hunter. He even told me of one instance where it had happened somewhere in southern Arizona. Then later, I heard about it from other sources also.

Obviously, he was well aware of the treasures of the KGC because in 1973, when I went hunting the first time for a KGC treasure at Glorieta Pass, New Mexico (as I mentioned before in my previous book about the KGC), I found that Bill already had a treasure hunting lease on the property. He also said to watch my back, because he believed that armed KGC sentinels were still on guard at some of the locations. In fact, I had been warned, or actually maybe threatened, a time or two in the past when it became known that I had been searching for the KGC treasures.

THE MYSTERIOUS DEATH OF FRANK FISH

Then, there are the rumors about the mysterious, untimely, and very sudden death of another old time treasure hunter, Frank L. Fish. He was originally from Los Angeles, and had, among other things, worked as an artist at same of the same aerospace companies that I had also worked for, so I have met a number of his friends who were all very suspicious about the circumstances surrounding his unexpected death at Amador City, California in 1963.

Frank was a pioneer in the field of treasure hunting. He usually was the very first to many sites with a metal detector which usually paid off with good results. So good in fact, that he open up a treasure museum in about 1955 at Amador City, California to show off his unique treasures to the public. He was exceptionally good at researching, then he would find the location where he often found treasure.

He eventually wrote a book, "BURIED TREASURES AND LOST MINES" in 1956 about these treasures and their 'supposedly' locations. I don't know if he was a devious man, or not, but I know that he was about most, or all, of these locations because I, like many others, bought the book and spent many hours and lots of gasoline trying to follow his information. I always found his directions were wrong—in fact, purposely wrong, so that no one following his information would ever find the locations. Even though I sometimes did find some of the roads, or washes, or creeks that he mentioned, they were not found where he said they were, and you could not get to his site from there—so finally, in disgust, I gave up, realizing that he never intended to reveal their true location to other treasure hunters. Besides, I knew that he was keeping secret many of his best locations, and I think that is what got him into trouble that led to some threats that he had complained about.

He never wrote publically about the KGC to my knowledge, but some think that he had some knowledge about some of their treasure, and was keeping this information about them, secret. I also had heard that he knew something about a secret society. It was known that he had a private diary (or a log book) full of information; and that, along with a lot of valuables, were missing when he was mysteriously found dead in his trailer house where he lived alone. He had mentioned numerous times to some people that his life had been threatened, and he was frightened.

People who knew him told me that Frank had much to live for, was in good health, had many plans for the future, and had just bought a new vehicle. That would not sound like some one about to committee suicide. Yet, the corners report said that it was--from poison. It was known that the night before he died, he had received a phone call that greatly disturbed him…Some believe that it could have been from someone wanting information in his secret logbook on the KGC.

IS THE LUE MAP ASSOCIATED WITH THE CONSTELLATIONS?

The following map of the constellations is something that I received years ago from my old friend, Shirley Estee Conaster. She was a cute little blond that when she put on a slinky red dress, you would never believe that she would also put on jeans and boots and hike into the Superstition Mountains to look for the famous lost Dutchman Mine, which she did numerous times. She had the heart of a true treasure hunter. In fact, it was her idea to start the "Prospectors Club of Southern California" back in about 1967. It is still the largest, as well as the oldest, treasure hunter's club in the world today. Unfortunately, she passed away a few years ago in Arizona where she had moved to be near her beloved Superstition Mountains.

Shirley had also been friends with Karl von Mueller for years. In fact, she had worked with him on numerous projects, including the LUE treasure, and I'm sure she had some inside information on it. If anyone could coax something like that from him, I know it would be her. She also commented that the map had been solved by three methods: algebraic, geometric, and astronomic.

Her comments, along with the map, were that this overall chart of the constellations (below) could easily apply to the LUE map, noting the similar shape of the ecliptic-curved line that occurs in both. I'm not sure that I see the connection, but maybe there is between the line and the arrangement of the major stars for any given month. I'm sure that she obtained this chart from Karl von Mueller.

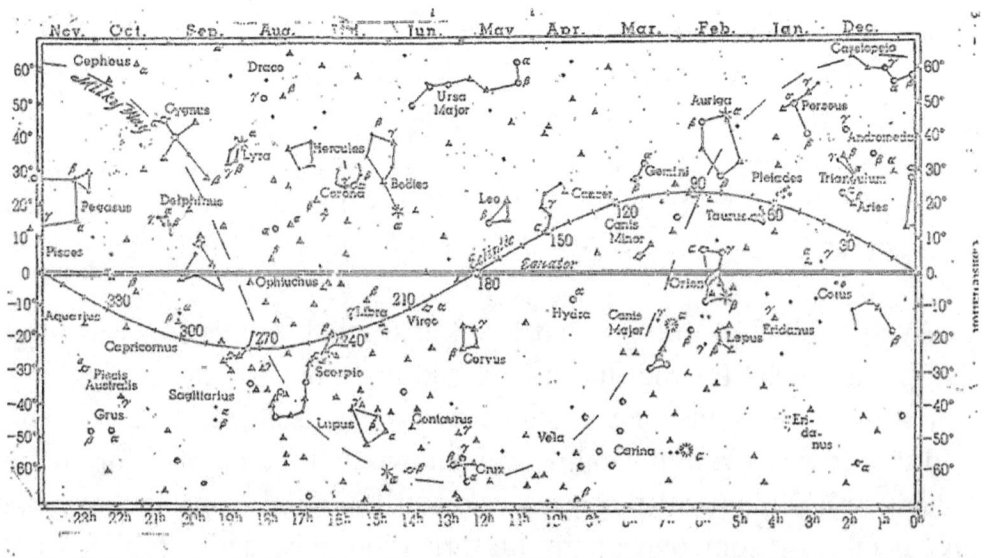

Chapter Seven

Update on Recent Searches For The KGC Treasure
By Roy Roush

Within the last few years, since the treasures of the Knights of the Golden Circle have become known, there has been a resurgence of treasure hunters looking for it. And although most treasure hunters are tightlipped about their activities or of finding treasure, some of them do let out some information, but I'm sure they don't tell all they really know.

One of the most recent and interesting stories appeared in an Oklahoma newspaper in May of 2005, in which two treasure hunters from Oklahoma (one by the name of Bud and the other Charlie who are both professional men) were hot on the trail of this treasure. In fact, they had been working on it for a number of years.

They say that the Confederacy never truly surrendered, and its leaders buried much treasure throughout North America, now estimated into the billions of dollars, for the day when the South would rise again. And that a lot of it was buried in Oklahoma and Northeast Texas to help finance a second Civil War, which they said that some of it has been found. They claim that the true story of the South has never been told, although some Southerners do know about it.

After many years of research, Bud claims that the famous Missouri outlaw, Jesse James, was a major member of the KGC, and much of his loot is now part of the KGC treasure, which includes gold and silver from the Confederacy treasure, donations from southern sympathizers, wartime raids on Northern banks and post war robberies.

No ledger or document has been found that details the extent of the hidden treasure, but they said they have uncovered evidence of an intricate, geometric grid system used to determine some of the locations across America. Some of the clues included Latin phrases and coded words, bent trees (referred to as "Hoot Owl" trees), rocks that had been shaped, etc; but the KGC had appointed armed sentries who knew the location of each site, protected it during their lifetime, then shared information with subsequent generations.

The two men had recently visited the summit of Blizzards Roost, a rocky hill near Cement, a small town about 65 miles South of Oklahoma City, where they described for different discoveries of buried treasure their since the early 1900's. They also pointed out coded messages and signs that had been carved into the rocks that were left as clues. The area had been Indian Territory at the time, so it offered many opportunities for good hideouts and burial sites.

Both men have spent considerable amounts of money in their pursuit of treasure, and have learned some hard lessons about sharing information with others. In one case, some other treasure hunters they befriended, went behind her backs, and unearthed one of the treasure sites, and all that Bud got was an 1880 silver dollar.

In another case, one of them had been asked by a landowner, who lived close to Rocky Point, to search his land with a metal detector. He found an old Wells Fargo safe buried under some cap rock, but was asked to leave before the safe was opened. He had reason to believe that it contained KGC money.

The two men are continuing their search by using newly acquired equipment, including night cameras to investigate some of the more rugged areas. One of the areas they are concentrating on is both sides of the Red River were they believe Jesse James hid some of his loot.

When asked if they have actually found any treasure, Bud replied that if he had, he wouldn't own up to it. However at last report, the men are still enjoying their hobby of pursuing treasure.

A LETTER TO THE Q&A DEPARTMENT

When I was answering the letters that were sent to the "Q&A Department of "TREASURE MAGAZINE" some years ago, here is a letter that I happened to find regarding a KGC treasure site:

Treasure Magazine
Van Nuys, California 91406

I have written to you before regarding a cache buried in Oklahoma. The details I had were sketchy, but I now have more accurate information. I would appreciate it if you could give me more information or refer me to the date that the article might have appeared in your magazine.

It is $80,000 in gold buried by a secret organization, the Knights of the

Golden Circle, in the Seven Devil's Mountains (now called Kiamichi Mtns.) 18 miles Northeast of Rattan & near Cloudy, Oklahoma. The cache is buried in a copper box in a cave in a rocky ledge, 1/2 mile east of

Captain T. M's-- (last name unknown) cabin.

Any information you can give me regarding this would be appreciated.

Thank you.
W.C., Berwyn, Illinois

Unfortunately, I had no information at the time to send him, and I still don't have anything specifically on it. Except that by now, perhaps what I have revealed in this book, and also in my previous one, would be of benefit.

KGC TREASURE BELIEVED AT WAPANUCKA, OKLAHOMA

It has been stated that Jesse James buried some of his loot in the little, and remote area of Wapanucka, which is in southeastern Oklahoma about 21 miles east of Tishomingo. The original site of Wapanucka is where the Chickasaw Indians (one of the original Five Civilized Tribes) established an academy in 1851.

It has been said that Albert Pike, an Arkansas attorney and a very prominent member of the KGC organization, secured a loyal following from the Five Civilized Tribes, which lends credence to the belief that some of the KGC treasures are buried in the area (which would include any buried by Jesse James.)

The academy is a ruined rubble of limestone now, but in 2003, the property was put up for auction, which led to an unusual string of events. A book had just been published by Bob Brewer and Warren Gettler, entitled "Shadow of the Sentinel." which is about Brewer's search for the hidden treasure of the KGC, that Brewer has dedicated most of his life to.

The book claimed that the property was littered with KGC treasure signs relating to a large cache of treasure buried there. So, partly to promote the book, some advertising appeared on local television stations and publications; and treasure hunters were invited to the property in order to promote the book and the legend of the KGC. However, there's been no actual evidence of treasure being found, only rumors. But one treasure expert, who had searched the property before the proposed sale, was convinced that a large KGC treasure was present.

Then followed a rather unusual and bizarre string of events. At the last-minute, just before the auction was to start, it was halted. There were numerous explanations. Some said it was because the property had been listed with another auction company, while others claimed because it had promoted Gettler's and Brewer's new book too much, but perhaps neither of those assertions were correct. Some said that the proposed sale was a joke in the first place.

The property had been listed as Jesse James's hideout. One of the parcels listed caves and carvings. Another parcel said it included various caves that were known to have been used by outlaws. The promoters of the sale explained that they were "Shooting for billions."

Treasure hunters from as far away as England and France journey to the area in hopes of purchasing a rich partial containing historic wealth, but when the auction was canceled just minutes before it was to begin, they, as well as others, were outraged and upset. The situation caused such a commotion that the two sisters, who had offered the land for sale, took shelter in a trailer with their attorney until the property had been cleared of all attendees.

Rumors were flying that the Vermont Stone Quarry Company had already purchased the property, but the two sisters had retained the right to treasure hunt. The treasure hunters felt they had been "sold out" and betrayed.

Then, the company hired a private investigator for protection. Later, a meteorologist from Hawaii was on the property looking for treasure. A rumor is that he found gold bars and sold them in Malaysia. But going back into the early history of the academy, there is evidence of another vast treasure being buried there that belonged to Col. Pittman Colbert, the President of the Chickasaw Council, and one of the wealthiest slave owners among the Chickasaws. It was claimed that when the Chickasaws moved from Mississippi to Oklahoma, Col. Colbert required a wagon and two mule teams to haul his gold to Indian Territory. It is believed that his gold was buried within yards of the academy site.

An interesting sidelight to the area is that when a report was made in 1859 of the staff members there, they happened to all be from states where the KGC was the most active, and most of the markings and signs on the property are attributed to the KGC. Then during the Civil War, the building served as a

Confederate hospital and prison, during which time, tunnels were dug from the basement of the academy to various sites around the property. And where better to hide treasure than in a tunnel?

It is also been claimed that Jesse James personally oversaw the burial of some of the KGC treasure at the academy, then added some of his own loot. It's also reported that in the 1930's, a city marshal from Rush Springs, Oklahoma found a buried cast-iron teakettle at Buzzards Roost, that is mentioned above, that contained several cryptic maps, including a map of the Wapanucka site that led to several small caches of coins, dating from the 1830s to 1880 by deciphering the map using Jesse James's personal treasure code.

So, it appears that historical evidence and the presence of numerous treasure markings indicate the possibility of a substantial treasure trove near the Wapanucka site that will undoubtedly draw treasure hunters to the area for decades to come.

CONCLUSION

Well, after spending a great deal of my life treasure hunting and gold prospecting, you might reasonable ask if I have found any treasure? My answer would have to be "Yes."

I have found one of the greatest of all treasures….It is the treasure of a world full of good memories, adventures, fellowship, and healthy living in the great outdoors—"Gods Great Cathedral!" And along the way, I have a few things to show, like a gold coin or two, lots of valuable old coins, jewelry, relics and a few gold nuggets that together would be equal to a sizable cache.

So my friends and readers, keep following that wonderful rainbow, for surely, you too can find treasure!

Note

This is my second book on the Knights of the Golden Circle and their treasures. The first book, published in March 2005, was entitled "THE MYSTERIOUS AND SECRET ORDER OF THE KNIGHTS OF THE GOLDEN CIRCLE" (ISBN Number 0-9723072-6-5) Web site: KnightsOfTheGoldenCircle.net.

It told of their early origins and purposes; their secret rites; how they influenced our early history and the Civil War; their plans to restart the war; and information on the huge treasures they buried around the country to finance a second war. It also told of some of their treasure sites where I went to search for it.

www.ingramcontent.com/pod-product-compliance
Lightning Source LLC
Chambersburg PA
CBHW060317240426

43661CB00059B/2789